IMPORTANT ★THINGS★ EVERY KID SHOULD KNOW TO SURVIVE MIDDLE SCHOOL

SANDY
SILVERTHORNE

HARVEST HOUSE PUBLISHERS
EUGENE, OREGON

Cover design by Dugan Design Group
Cover photos © New Africa, kasheev / Fotolia

HARVEST KIDS is a trademark of The Hawkins Children's LLC. Harvest House Publishers, Inc., is the exclusive licensee of the trademark HARVEST KIDS.

A huge thank you to Mark Lemaire, Matt Erdmann, their middle school groups, and all the middle schoolers at Willamette Christian School for all their input and help with this book.

**Important Things Every Kid Should Know to Survive Middle School**
Copyright © 2020 by Sandy Silverthorne
Published by Harvest House Publishers
Eugene, Oregon 97408
www.harvesthousepublishers.com

ISBN 978-0-7369-7657-2 (pbk.)
ISBN 978-0-7369-7658-9 (eBook)

Library of Congress Cataloging-in-Publication Data is on file at the Library of Congress, Washington, DC.

**Printed in the United States of America**

20 21 22 23 24 25 26 27 28 / BP-AR / 10 9 8 7 6 5 4 3 2 1

# Contents

Important Things Every Kid Should Know About...

# 1

Important Things Every Kid Should Know About...

## Thriving in Middle School
### You Can Do This

Welcome to the only book you'll ever need not only to *survive* middle school but to be spectacular in it! This book is crammed with amazing tips to help you be a success at your new school in every way. You'll learn important stuff about making friends, choosing classes, and trying out for a sport. Need help with homework, finding your way around the school, or deciding what to eat before a test? No problem. We've also got some great ideas on making good decisions, dealing with temptations, and knowing which foods to avoid in the cafeteria.

You'll find a few little personality quizzes to help you figure out what's right for you when doing your homework, choosing extra-curricular activities, and more. Feel free to write in the book as you take the quizzes—after all, they're all for you! We also have a few sections called "Raising Your Parents." Share these with your mom and dad to help them know what's going on in your world.

Each chapter ends with a section called "Checking In." It includes a Bible verse, a few thoughts about how to apply it to your life, and a short prayer.

So get ready to know more about God, more about yourself, and more about what to expect in this crazy world called middle school.

If somebody gave you this book, this might be the first time you've ever thought much about God. That's totally cool. After all, you can't see Him or just call Him on your cell phone. And let's face it, if He does exist, He's got to be ginormous, so you might wonder why He would be interested in listening to you or care about you. Well, the truth is, God does care about you. In fact, He probably arranged for you to pick up this book! His number one priority is getting to know you and becoming friends with you. Seriously! You're at the top of His list of things to think about. In fact, He loves you so much He even took care of the one thing that's been keeping people away from Him. We'll explore that later.

So let's get started! Let's find out how you can survive and even thrive in middle school!

## How Do You Feel About Middle School?

As you get ready to dive into this new adventure of middle school, it's probably important to figure out how you're feeling about the whole thing. Are you excited? Nervous? Somewhere in between the two? Well, here's your first little unscientific quiz to figure out how you're feeling about middle school. Just check the phrase below that best describes how you're feeling as you get ready to make this change.

☐ Really excited! New friends, different classes, sports, music, drama...I'm finally starting to grow up!

☐ Kind of happy but not sure what to expect. Are the eighth graders really that big?

☐ Kind of curious. What classes should I take? Will I have lunch with my friends? What if I get lost? What activities should I do this year? What if I forget my locker combination? I've got lots of questions.

☐ HELP! Whose idea was this anyway? I'm moving to Argentina!

If you checked the fourth option, thanks for your honesty. (Although, come to think of it, Argentina probably has middle schools too.) If the idea of middle school is scary for you, remember that you're not alone. Change is hard for everybody—even adults. It usually means leaving something comfortable, something you're used to—like elementary school—and stepping into something a little more unknown. Everybody gets nervous about something. A lot of people don't show it, but they are nervous. But trust us, in a couple of days or weeks, you'll get so used to the middle school routine that it will start to feel totally comfortable. In fact, you'll probably be helping other kids figure stuff out. If you have a lot of questions, don't worry—this book will answer almost all of them.

## How to Get Over Middle School Phobia

It's not unusual to be a little curious or even a little nervous about the transition to middle school. After all, you've been in elementary school for five or six years. You've gotten used to the routine. You have one teacher all day long, you're at the same desk, you work on some math or spelling or history, and then you have recess and lunch, and before long, it's time to head home. Simple, huh? But now they're throwing this middle school thing at you. There are so many unknowns.

But hey, you've got this. You're going to be great! If you find yourself a little nervous about the whole thing, here are some quick tips that will help lower your anxiety level. In fact, these ideas can help you no matter what you're nervous about.

**1. Keep moving!** Did you know that running around, playing soccer, or riding your bike is not only good for your body but also good for your brain? If you're feeling worried or anxious about something, try exercising a little bit. Go for a jog or a walk with the dog. Shoot some hoops. Even a little bit of exercise will help your body calm down.

**2. Get some sleep.** Are you a morning person or a night owl? Either way, make sure you get at least nine hours of sleep each night. Getting in this habit will help you function at your best and feel less anxiety. Sounds good, huh?

**3. Please (don't) pass the cookies.** We all love sweets, but sometimes sugar can give you even *more* anxiety. Yikes—don't want that! If you're dealing with anxiety, try to cut down on sugary sweets as well as foods with caffeine—pop, coffee, tea, and even chocolate. And remember to drink lots of water. Your body (and your feelings!) will thank you for it.

**4. Fun in the sun!** Believe it or not, getting 15 to 30 minutes of sunlight every day will help your body feel calmer. So go outside and soak up some sun! Just make sure to put on sunscreen so you don't get burned.

**5. Alone, please.** Having some downtime every day is a great way to make the switch back to school at the end of summer. Take an hour to sit and read or listen to an audiobook all by yourself. Why don't you take some time to draw? Or write stories? Or read a chapter from your Bible? Being alone at least once a day is a great way to keep your body and emotions cool and calm.

**6. Talk it out.** One of the best ways to relieve your anxiety (and to realize that you're not the only one who feels anxious sometimes) is to talk to somebody about it. Find an adult—your mom or dad, a teacher, a youth pastor—and tell them what you're feeling. Just sharing with another person is a good step to getting rid of your nervousness.

**7. One more thing.** If you're still feeling anxious, try this calming exercise. Breathe in slowly and deeply for four seconds. (To breathe deeply, think of the air going all the way down to the bottom of your lungs.) Hold your breath for four seconds. Then let it out slowly for four seconds. Wait another four, and then do it all again. Take your time, breathe slowly, and count. Doing that three or four times when you're feeling stressed will help your body calm down. A lot.

## Checking In: *No Worries*

*Don't worry about anything; instead, pray about everything; tell God your needs, and don't forget to thank him for his answers. If you do this, you will experience God's peace, which is far more wonderful than the human mind can understand.*

Philippians 4:6-7

The Bible was written more than 2,000 years ago. It's been read by millions or billions of people, and there, right in the middle of the New Testament, it says not to worry about anything. Now, if it seems important enough for God to put that in the Bible, then it seems that maybe lots of people need to hear it.

The truth is, almost everybody in the world tends to get anxious about something. We worry, fret, and obsess about things. And a lot of these things never even end up happening. So in other words, you're not the only person who is worrying about stuff.

Are you nervous about a new school, making friends, homework, getting on a team, or maybe even remembering your locker combination? Well, the cool thing about the verse you just read is that it tells us *what to do* when we're feeling anxious or worried about something. It says to let God know what's going on. Pray. Just let Him know about whatever it is that's bothering you.

Then the verse says to thank Him. Thank Him for what He's already done for you and maybe even thank Him that He's going to get you through this thing you're worried about.

And then comes the promise: He'll give you peace—His peace. He might not take the problem away—maybe He'll let you go through it—but He does promise to be with you and to give you peace for the journey.

**Extra Credit:** Read Matthew 6:25-34 and see what Jesus says about worrying. He says that God knows all about what's going on with you and will take care of everything you need.

> Dear Lord, you know how worried I am about
> _____. Would You help me with that? Help
> me go around it or through it or whatever You
> want, but please be with me and give me Your
> peace as we experience this together. Amen.

# 2

## Getting Ready
### Beating Middle School Phobia
### Before It Begins

One of the things that makes going into new things kind of scary is that there are so many unknowns. And going to middle school might have lots of those. What if I get lost going to class? How will I know where things are? Will I make any friends? What if I forget my homework—or even worse, my lunch? How big is the place, and where are the bathrooms? You know, important stuff like that. So here are a couple of ways to get ready for your new school before the school year even starts. Give one or two of these a try.

## How to Beat Middle School Phobia Before It Starts

1. During the spring before you leave elementary school, while classes are still in session, head over to your new school with your parents. Make sure you check in with the office first. Walk around and find out where stuff is, like the cafeteria. Check out where the gym, the library, and some of the classrooms are located. If possible, get a teacher or student to show you around. Just being there might take some of the mystery out of things.

2. Draw a map of the school showing all the places you need to be—classrooms, bike racks, science lab, library, cafeteria...and don't forget the bathrooms!

3. Grab some friends and shoot a video about your adventures at middle school. You could make it like a news report, or it could be a comedy about a new kid at school who keeps getting lost. You could even make a monster movie—*The Man-Eating Tuna Casserole from the School Cafeteria*. Use costumes, write a script, and add some special effects. (It's probably best to do this on a weekend so the school staff won't think you're a bunch of weirdos.)

4. Set some goals for the upcoming school year. Sometimes when you choose a few things you'd like to make happen, you feel a little more in control, and some of the fear goes away. Make your goals realistic but challenging. Maybe you'd like to make all As and Bs. Or try out for track. Or make two new friends the first week. Or enter a science fair. What are some goals you'd like to meet this year at school? Write down three or four.

_____

_____

_____

## Who I Am: My Likes, Goals, and Interests

After a few weeks in middle school, you'll notice that groups will start to develop more than they did in elementary school. And that's okay because you'll begin to find friends who are interested in the same things you are, like Star Wars, endangered species, math, or robots. So what are you like? Take this little quiz and find out. Just put a check mark by each one that describes you.

☐ **Cool kid.** You know all the latest songs and the latest dance moves. You know how to talk so you sound...well, cool. You know what looks right, sounds right, and just *is* right.

☐ **Jock.** You're the MVP no matter what sport you play—basketball, soccer, double Dutch...even Ping-Pong.

☐ **Computer nerd.** You're the kid who codes and knows what "graphical user interface" means. You've also probably beaten a few *Need for Speed* video games.

☐ **Drama star.** You can jump up in front of a crowd and sing, dance, act, or give an ad-libbed speech with no preparation and no fear.

☐ **Musician.** You love to listen to or dance to any kind of music (except polka). Maybe you like to sing and are getting good at playing an instrument too.

☐ **A student.** Not just "a student," but an A student. It's nothing for you to get all As on your report card. You love to learn, and good grades just come naturally to you.

☐ **Artsy person.** You love being creative. You like to draw, sew, sculpt, paint, or design. You hear this all the time: "Wow, how do you do that? I can't even draw a straight line!"

☐ **Introvert.** This doesn't mean you're shy or withdrawn. It's just you get energized by ideas. It wouldn't bother you to be alone for hours just coming up with some cool and creative solutions to life's problems. You might even be an artsy person or even a jock and an introvert at the same time.

☐ **Extrovert.** You get energized by being around people. When you've spent too much time alone, you feel tired and a little down.

Do any of those describe you? Middle school will give you tons of opportunities to explore things you're interested in. We'll talk more about fun classes and after-school clubs in the next couple of chapters.

## Checking In: *What Do They Want from Me?*

*Do to others what you would have them do to you.*
Matthew 7:12 NIV

Every school has some rules of behavior they expect everybody else to follow. Be nice to people, don't litter, don't skateboard through the library during school hours...the normal stuff. Check out your school's rules of behavior—they're usually on the school's website. We've listed some of the common ones down below. One thing you'll probably notice is that your school's rules of conduct look a lot like the way God wants us to act toward other people all the time. Check out the list, and notice the Bible verses right next to each one—God is way ahead of your school. And He wants us to treat one another right. After all, you're one of His kids.

Here are some of the things you'll probably find in your school's rules of behavior:

- *Don't threaten or bully anyone, online or in person.* Treat people the way you'd like them to treat you, just like the Bible verse above says.

- *Don't steal stuff.* This is a no-brainer. Don't take other people's things—they need them. "You must not steal" (Exodus 20:15).

- *Don't put people down.* Nobody likes being made fun of. You don't have to talk all unicorns and roses but speak positively to other people. "Keep your mouth closed and you'll stay out of trouble" (Proverbs 21:23).

- *Show respect for other people.* Adults, parents, other kids, coaches, teachers...you get the idea. "Don't be conceited, sure of your own wisdom. Instead, trust and reverence the Lord" (Proverbs 3:7).

- *Watch your language.* Yeah, choose not to swear—it makes you sound dumb. You'll probably hear a lot more profanity in middle school because kids think it makes them sound cool. It doesn't. "If anyone can control his tongue, it proves he has perfect control over himself in every other way" (James 3:2). Hmm...that makes a lot of sense.

- *Dress appropriately.* You don't have to spend a lot of money or wear the latest style, but take care of yourself. Make sure that you look (and smell!) clean and that your clothes don't look all run down. "Christian women [and boys and girls!] should be noticed for being kind and good, not for the way they fix their hair or because of their jewels or fancy clothes" (1 Timothy 2:9).

Simple, huh? It all goes back to the first command on our list—treat people the way you'd like them to treat you. If this is hard for you, or if there are certain people in your life that push your buttons, ask God to help you with your attitude toward them. He'll give you patience and wisdom to know how to deal with them.

> Dear Lord, most of the rules at my school are easy to follow, but I might have some trouble with a couple of them. Would You please help me with _____ and _____ and always help me remember to treat other people the way I want to be treated? In Jesus's name, amen.

It was becoming apparent that it was time
for Jacob to clean out his locker.

# 3

## The First Day of School
### Lockers, Classes, Homeroom, and What's for Lunch

Wow, you made it—the first day of school! You've already checked out the place, got your class schedule, figured out where things are, and gotten familiar with the rules of conduct. You've got your books, supplies, lunch...now what?

### How Do I Get There?

There are tons of ways to get to your new middle school. Your mom or dad might drop you off, or you might walk, ride a school bus, or even skateboard your way down there. So you really have no excuse not to go. Here are a couple transportation ideas you might consider for getting to school.

*School bus.* If you choose to ride the school bus, make sure you're at the bus stop right on time (or even a little early) every morning. Most bus drivers don't wait for stragglers. And always be cool on the bus—do what the driver tells you and don't harass the other kids.

If you ride your bike or skateboard to school, you might wonder, what do I do with it once I get there?

*Bike.* Most schools have bike racks or a bike cage where you can leave your bike for the day. Even if your bike is in the cage, make sure you bring a good lock for it and lock it up before you go to class. You can get the best bike locks at bicycle or sporting goods stores. Make sure you lock your bike every time you leave it anywhere. That way it'll always be there when you get back.

*Skateboard.* Most schools have rules about skateboarding on school property, so they'll want you to leave your skateboard either in your locker or in the bike cage for the day. So don't picture yourself skating from class to class all day long like in the movies. Ain't gonna happen.

When you arrive at school, the first thing you'll notice is how big the place seems. The campus is a lot bigger than your elementary school was, there are a lot more kids here, and some of them are a lot bigger than you expected. Some of them look older than the teachers! And everybody seems to know what they're doing! Don't worry, you got this. Let's go through a typical day of middle school. Ready?

## Homeroom

Usually this is your first class of the day, and it sort of jump-starts things. Since you'll be going to different classes throughout the day, think of homeroom as your base camp. The teacher will take roll to see if you're there. (If you aren't, where are you?) They'll give you announcements about sports tryouts, special events coming up, and maybe what's for lunch in the cafeteria that day. Usually this class isn't very long, and then you'll be on your way. And speaking of that, there's...

## Passing Period

This is the time allowed for you to pass from one class to another. It's usually about five minutes. Sometimes it's super easy to get from one class to another on time because they're right next door to each other. But occasionally, your next class seems like it's on the other side of the planet, so you might not have time to do anything but drop by your locker to pick up a book you need.

## Your Locker

Speaking of lockers, most middle schools will assign you one. Lockers are cool because you can store stuff there rather than carrying it around all day long. You can keep your notebook, textbooks, and lunch in your locker until you need them. You'll probably be assigned one when you register for school. You may have to supply your own lock, or maybe the lock will be built-in. If it's built-in, the school will give you the combination. If you have to buy your own lock, the combination will be included in the package.

"Wait—what if I forget my locker combination? What will happen to me? Will it be a disaster?" No, not really. Just cruise on down to the office, and they'll look it up for you. But a good idea is to keep your combination written down somewhere for a couple of days, like in your notebook or in your wallet. Then after a while, you'll know it by heart. In fact, you'll be able to work your combination in your sleep, which is a good thing in case you fall asleep at school on a Monday morning.

## Five Ways to Make Your Locker Truly Memorable

1. Install surround-sound speakers inside so every time you open it up, the Avengers theme blasts through the hall.

2. Design a miniature golf course to fit inside your locker. Consider a miniature bowling alley next year.

3. Put a folding lawn chair in there so you can relax a bit between classes.

4. Install a chocolate fountain. Bring graham crackers, strawberries, or pound cake for easy and delicious dipping.

5. Design a life-size cutout of yourself and place it outside your locker to guard it while you're at class.

### *Make It Your Own!*

One of the cool things about having a locker is that you can decorate it to fit your unique personality. Put up pictures of your family,

your pets, a movie, or sports stars you like. Or you can get creative and decorate for the various seasons. Hobby Lobby and other craft stores even have magnetic shelves, frames, and wallpaper to give your locker that special touch.

Don't use glue or permanent markers to decorate your locker. Since the school reassigns lockers every year, the next person to use it might not want photos of your family, pet iguana, or BFF in there.

## Class Schedule

Now it's time to figure out what classes you're going to take. Wait, what? Why do they do that? Well, in middle school, you'll take different classes from teachers who specialize in their own subjects. This helps you learn a lot more about the subjects you're studying.

So how do you know what classes to take? Don't worry; there are counselors at the school who will help you with that. Your school might have somebody connect with you before school starts, or they might send you your class schedule before the first day. You'll probably have five to seven classes throughout the day, including homeroom and maybe a study hall (which is where you can do a lot of your homework).

Some schools have a rotating schedule, so you don't have the same classes every day. You might have the same classes on Mondays, Wednesdays, and Fridays and a different set of classes on Tuesdays and Thursdays. It might sound confusing, but don't sweat it—it's simpler than it sounds. Here's an example:

| Monday, Wednesday, Friday | Tuesday, Thursday |
|---|---|
| homeroom | homeroom |
| math | science |
| English and history block | foreign language |
| lunch | lunch |
| tech/computers | PE |
| study hall | choir |

## What to Bring to Class

Your teachers will tell you what to bring to class—which books and which supplies you'll need, like a notebook, paper, and pens and pencils. Most of the time, you and your parents will get a list of supplies a few weeks before school starts, or the list might be on your school's website. If you can't find it anywhere, just raise your hand and ask your teacher what you need to bring.

Here's a generic list of supplies. See if you can figure out which ones are fake.

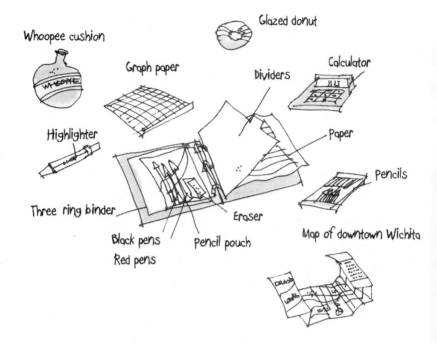

Whoopee cushion
Glazed donut
Graph paper
Dividers
Calculator
Highlighter
Paper
Pencils
Three ring binder
Eraser
Black pens
Red pens
Pencil pouch
Map of downtown Wichita

## Raising Your Parents: Let's Go Shopping!

Here's an idea you might try a couple of weeks before school starts. Find out what supplies you're going to need by checking your school's website. If they don't have a list on there, go down to the school and ask for a list of supplies from the people in the office. The folks who work in the office are probably nice, and they'll be impressed that you're thinking about this ahead of time. After you get the list, go to your mom or dad and say, "Okay, it's time to get some school supplies. Mustn't wait until the last minute." This will show your parents you're a kind and responsible soon-to-be middle schooler.

And while you're out there shopping for supplies, why not stop for a burger or a shake or something? School shopping can make you hungry. Who knew getting school supplies could be so much fun?

Okay, back to your school day...

## Lunchtime

As the morning passes, you'll suddenly find yourself at lunchtime! This is a great time of day. Your chance to catch your breath, hang out with friends, and enjoy a peanut butter sandwich and some Fritos. Here's one thing to be aware of—there may be more than one lunch period at your school, so you might not end up eating with your friends. If this happens, you can do one of three things:

1. Find some new friends to eat with. Who knows? You might discover some cool people you never would have met before.

2. Disguise yourself as a giant bologna sandwich and sneak into the lunch period that you want. Make sure your friends realize it's you so they don't end up eating you by mistake.

3. Talk to your school counselor to see if you might juggle your schedule so you can be around your friends at lunchtime. If this doesn't work this term or semester, see if you can make it work the next time around.

### What's for Lunch? The Cafeteria

The few, the proud, the cafeteria diners. You might bring your own lunch—you know, sandwich, chips, carrots, and a cookie—or you might eat the school lunch. You may have heard rumors that school lunches are bad, but actually, they are much better than they used to be. Schools often feature good stuff, like pizza, cheeseburgers, deli sandwiches, and soup. Also, you might be able to find lots of à la carte items (that means you can choose the ones you want), like salads, fries, corn dogs, tacos, burritos, or tater tots. Sound good?

### After Lunch

Lunchtime is usually 30 or 45 minutes long, and then it's time to get back to work. Stop by your locker, swap out some books, and you're off. You'll probably have two or three classes after lunch, depending on how your school operates. It'll work just the same as it did in the morning. You'll be in class for about an hour and then move on to the next one. Pretty simple all in all. Class, passing period, locker, class.

Look at that! You made it through the whole day. Easy, wasn't it?

> ### Helpful Tip: Plan Your Day Right
>
> If you can, schedule your fun classes—art, drama, music, PE—after lunch. That makes the day go easier, and it'll be a lot more fun.

### I Miss Recess!

One thing you'll notice about middle school is that there's no recess. We're not sure who came up with that idea, but it's an inconvenient fact you'll just have to live with. But here's the good news: With passing periods, lunch, and other breaks, you'll have plenty of opportunity to get up, move around, and talk with your friends. And you can get your energy out during PE—we'll talk more about that a little bit later.

## Checking In: *The Lord Made This Day!*

*This is the day the LORD has made. We will
rejoice and be glad in it.*

Psalm 118:24 NLT

Sometimes it's hard to get up in the morning, isn't it? When the alarm goes off or Mom says, "Time to get up!" sometimes you'd rather do anything than let your feet hit the floor.

But today's verse tells us that this day is special. It says that God made this day. It's not an accident. It's not just that the earth rotated one more time or that 24 hours have passed. God made this day with you in mind. So what do we do?

For one thing, start by being thankful to God. Try thinking of five things you're thankful for, such as air or the fact that you have a bed or the breakfast you're about to eat or your family.

Next, decide to be happy. That's what "rejoice" means. Choose to be glad it's today!

The next thing you can try is to look for the little things God might do for you as you go through the day. You might meet a new person. You might start to understand math! Or maybe the cafeteria will have something good on their menu today—who knows? This is the day that God made, so enjoy it!

**Extra Credit:** Take a couple minutes right now and write down five things you're thankful for.

_____

_____

_____

_____

_____

Dear Lord, thanks that this day isn't an accident or something that just happened by chance. Thanks that You made it and that I can be thankful all day long and that I can even enjoy it. Even if I'm tired or bored, help me see what You're up to in my life and in the lives of the people around me. In Jesus's name, amen.

# 4

Important Things Every Kid Should Know About...

## Electives
### Robotics, Spanish, Drawing, and Cooking

Question: What do all of the above have in common?
Answer: You might be taking one of them this term.

One way middle school is different from elementary school is that you'll get to take some different kinds of classes that interest you. Of course, there are some classes that everybody has to take, like math, English, history, and science. But in middle school, you'll also get to choose some classes in other subjects you're interested in. These are called *electives*. Electives range from robotics to drama to art and even popular music. Here are just a few of the classes your school might offer. See if some of these look interesting.

*Art*

Do you like to draw, or would you like to learn? Or paint with watercolors or oil paints? How about making cool pots and bowls out of clay? If this sounds like you, you might want to consider taking some art classes. Sometimes classes in art will cover everything—drawing, painting, ceramics, and so on—or you might be able to specialize in one or two kinds of art.

Check it out. You might be the next Picasso. If you don't know who that is, Google him. He painted some weird stuff. But if you enjoy the visual arts and creating stuff with your hands, check out an art class.

## Drama

Most middle schools feature classes in drama, and we're not talking about the kind of drama you get in the school hallway: "Did you hear that Allison isn't talking to Maddie anymore because she heard she was gossiping about her to Kyle?" No, we're talking about doing plays—learning lines, blocking (where you move onstage), and even being in produc-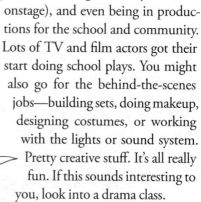tions for the school and community. Lots of TV and film actors got their start doing school plays. You might also go for the behind-the-scenes jobs—building sets, doing makeup, designing costumes, or working with the lights or sound system. Pretty creative stuff. It's all really fun. If this sounds interesting to you, look into a drama class.

## Shop Class

Do you like to work with your hands? Are you good at fig-uring out mechanical things and fixing stuff? Are you interested in drafting, electronics, or even architecture? Then a shop class might be just what you want. In these classes, you'll be able to work on projects in wood or metal or even learn how to work with elec-tronics. And don't think this stuff is just for boys. If you're a girl and activities like these interest you, sign up for a shop class. You'll love it. And in a lot of the classes, at the end of the term, you'll have a cool project that you made all by yourself.

## Foreign Language

*Parlez vous francais? ¿Habla español?* Do you speak French? Do you speak Spanish? You might be able to answer yes to these and many other non-English questions if you sign up for a foreign language class. Lots of schools offer Spanish, French, German, or even Japanese. In a couple of years, you might sound like a native speaker. After a while, get a movie in the language you're taking and see how well you understand it.

### Culinary Arts

That sounds fancy, doesn't it? It actually means cooking and serving food. A lot of schools have culinary arts programs where you can learn how to gather ingredients, follow a recipe, and prepare cool meals, such as grilled salmon with twice-baked potatoes, roasted asparagus, and chocolate mousse (pronounced *moose*) for dessert. If this is making you hungry, you might consider checking out a culinary arts class.

Josh had a bad feeling that his Culinary Arts grades were on the skids.

### Band or Orchestra

Are you musical? Or would you like to be? Middle school is a great chance to explore and improve your already impressive musical talent. Almost every middle school (well, maybe not the ones in Antarctica) offers orchestra or band. So get in there! Learn how to play the trumpet or violin or tuba. Research shows that kids who play musical instruments get better grades and do better in their studies. And they're a lot stronger too if they have to carry the bass drum in the marching band.

### Choir

If you like to sing, you've got to get in the choir. If your school has a choir class as an elective, you'll find it's a great way to meet people, have fun, learn music, and maybe even travel a little bit. Lots of schools enter choir competitions with other schools, so you can go and show off your amazing vocal skills. As a bonus, you'll get some music education, and your voice will get better too.

### Robotics

More and more middle schools are starting robotics classes and clubs. You'll get to design, build, and even program your own robots. So cool. Maybe you can design one that'll do your homework or run laps for you in PE! (Probably not.) You might enjoy getting together with some other "robot heads" and creating some amazing projects. If your school doesn't feature robotics, gather some friends and a willing teacher and start your own robotics club after school.

### Filmmaking

Do you dream of writing, directing, or starring in a movie? Then you definitely need to take a filmmaking class. In this class, you'll learn how to stage a scene, light it, work with your actors, shoot it, and then go back and edit it. Then add sound, music, and special effects. Soon, you'll be hosting your own world premiere!

### Newspaper and Yearbook

Do you like to gather the news and write about it? Joining the school newspaper staff will be excellent for you. Most school newspapers need writers, illustrators, photographers, reporters, and editors. If you like bigger projects and you're into writing, photography, and graphic design, check out becoming a member of your school's yearbook staff. And a lot of schools nowadays get their news out with a student-produced TV news broadcast every morning that goes throughout the school. You also might see whether your school has an online newspaper you can write or blog for.

### Technology

Many middle schools require this class to get you feeling comfortable on the computer. Your school might even have some advanced computer classes that include making PowerPoint presentations, working with Photoshop and InDesign, programming, and even some video or music editing. Check it out!

All in all, things will probably be a lot more interesting in middle school than they were in elementary school. You'll have more choices, more opportunities, and way more chances to try new things. The key is to find something you like or are interested in and then *have fun!*

Check out your school's website to find out which of these classes they offer. Then make sure you get one or more of them on your schedule. If your school doesn't offer a class or club in the subject you're interested in, grab a few like-minded friends, talk to a teacher, and see if you can start an after-school club.

If you're feeling adventurous, try something you've never tried before. Take guitar lessons or learn how to play Ultimate Frisbee. Take a biology class or try some creative writing. Take a lesson from Heisman quarterback Tim Tebow—he switched from football to baseball a couple of years ago and is having a blast.

## Raising Your Parents: Make It a Date

Are you still having trouble deciding what classes you'd like to take? Here's an idea: Make a date with one or both of your parents—go out to breakfast or go for ice cream—and talk to them about it. If they've been paying attention for the past 11 years, they'll know a lot about you. Sometimes other people see things in our lives and personalities that we might not even be aware of ourselves. They might have some good ideas of classes or activities for you to check out.

And you get a breakfast or ice cream while you're at it. That sounds like a win-win.

---

### Checking In: *Where Do I Fit?*

*I will praise You, for I am fearfully and wonderfully made.*

Psalm 139:14 NKJV

Psalm 139 says that you are "fearfully and wonderfully made." In other words, you're not an accident! You might not feel that way all the time, but it's true. God knew you before you were even born! He knows what you like (movies, music, football, new shoes) and what you don't like (Brussels sprouts, homework, tests, liverwurst). So when you're deciding which classes and after-school activities to get involved with, take a look at yourself and see what kinds of things you like and are good at.

Are you an amazing volleyball or football player? Go for it. Try out for the team. Do you like being in front of people? Try drama or music. Maybe your school has a 4-H club, where you can take care of animals. Are you a science whiz or good at chess? Your school might have a class or a club just for you. God gave you the gifts, skills, and talents you possess, and He loves to see you using them for Him!

**Extra Credit:** Read Psalm 37:4. You'll find a command and a promise. Check it out.

> Dear Lord, thank You for giving me the gifts, talents, and skills I have. Especially thank You for making me good at _____. Thank You for the new opportunities I'll find in middle school, and help me know where I fit and the places where I can shine. In Jesus's name, amen.

Jason had a bad feeling about his new PE class.

# 5

## PE
### The Next-Best Thing to Recess

We mentioned middle school is going to mean the end of recess. "Aughhh! That was my favorite part of the entire day!" you exclaim. But in middle school, the next-best thing to recess is PE (physical education). Now we're not sure how much actual *education* goes on here, but it is a chance to get out and run around a little bit. It is as long as your other classes, but that includes a little time at the beginning to change into your spiffy PE school uniform and again at the end to take a shower. More on that later.

## Conditioning

In PE, you might get to try out fun new sports, like flag football, tennis, softball, basketball, and soccer. And chances are you'll learn how to do a little conditioning—push-ups, pull-ups, jogging, and so on. So here are some hints on how to succeed.

### Push-Ups

It might be a good idea to practice push-ups at home before you start PE class. Just lie down on your stomach on the floor with your arms out from your shoulders (figure A). Then push up until your arms are straight (figure B). Guess that's where the name "push-up"

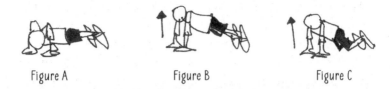

Figure A                    Figure B                    Figure C

came from—go figure. Now lower yourself to the ground. Then do it again. Simple.

You might be able to do these with no problem, or you might find them a little challenging. If you're having trouble doing these, here's a little hack that will help—"cheat pushups." Try doing them with your knees down on the floor (figure C). Then lower yourself down and do as many of these as you can. Do these cheat pushups every day and soon you'll be doing the real thing. As that happens, do several cheat pushups and then sneak in a real one every now and then. Soon, you'll be able to do a bunch of the real ones.

## Pull-Ups

You start a pull-up by hanging on a bar with your arms about shoulder-width apart. Then you pull yourself up until your chin is over the bar. These are hard for almost everybody. So if you can't do one of these, try this. Find a bar, maybe in the gym or on a playground. Jump up onto the bar until your chin is over it. (Careful, don't hit it!) Then lower yourself down. It's like you're doing a pulldown. But lower yourself slowly. That strengthens your arms and shoulders, so after a while, you'll be able to pull yourself up. By the way, your PE teacher isn't going to be all that impressed with your pull-downs. But keep at it for a month or so, and soon you'll be able to do some pull-ups!

## Take a Lap

Just like push-ups and pull-ups, running is something you should ease into. If you've been active playing basketball or riding your bike, you might be in good shape already, and running a couple of laps will be a piece of cake. But if you've been lying on the couch a lot, binge-watching your favorite TV shows or playing video games for hours at a time, you might need to start slowly.

Try running a short distance—like to the kitchen (just kidding). Try jogging around the block or down the street. Or if there's a track near where you live, try running slowly around it once or even halfway around. Go as far as you can before it starts getting hard to breathe, and then stop and walk a bit. Then try to go a little farther tomorrow. Do this every day, and in a few days or weeks, you'll be in much better shape, and you'll be ready to run as many laps as your PE teacher assigns.

Here are a couple of things to remember: First, make sure it's okay with your doctor for you to exercise. And second, get some decent running shoes and try to run on grass or dirt or a track if you can. Running on the street can be hard on your knees and feet.

## Stylin' in Your PE Uniform

Chances are you'll need to wear a nifty uniform for your PE class. You wouldn't want to run around and slide into third in your Old Navy shirt and Mid-rise Sateen Rockstar jeans. The school will tell you what to get and even where to get it. The uniform usually

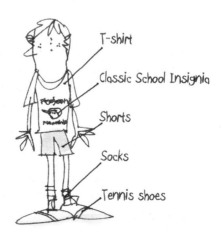

Please (boys especially) remember to take your PE uniform home and wash it every week. If you don't, before too long, it'll be able to stand up on its own.

consists of a T-shirt and cool shorts. You'll love them. And you'll probably need tennis shoes of some kind.

### Showers: A New Frontier

Most of the time, your PE class is going to wrap up early enough for you to shower and get ready for your next class. "What? Nobody told me I'd have to be showering with 30 other kids in the middle of my school day! Awkward."

It might be awkward the first few times, especially for sixth graders, but after a while, it'll become somewhat natural. Most middle schools provide a nice industrial-grade towel to use to dry off. So just jump in, rinse off, dry off, and get dressed. It can be quite refreshing. After your shower, you'll feel better and smell better, and the kids who sit next to you in your next class will thank you for not stinking.

## Checking In: *Just the Way You Are*

*Haven't you yet learned that your body is the home of the Holy Spirit God gave you, and that He lives within you?*

1 Corinthians 6:19

When you turn 11 or 12, you're going to start noticing changes in your body. That's how God designed it—your body is getting ready to grow up and become an adult. Don't worry, you won't be an adult for several more years, but your body is getting prepared. And according to the Scripture you just read, God's Spirit lives inside of you.

Middle school can be a time when you don't like how your body looks. You might think you're too heavy or too skinny or too tall or too short or you've got zit problems or your hair gets all greasy or whatever. And on top of all that, some kids might even tell you that your body doesn't measure up. Nowadays that's called "body shaming," and it's not right. It's not true, either.

Did you know that God loves you just the way you are? Skinny, heavy, with zits or crazy hair—don't listen to the voices out there. Remember that God isn't as concerned as we are with our outward appearance—He looks at our hearts (read 1 Samuel 16:7). If you feel like you'd like to lose weight or get in better shape, that's awesome, but remember, God loves you no matter what shape you're in.

**Extra Credit:** Read 1 Samuel 16:3-7 to see how God sees people differently than people see people.

> Dear Lord, You know the areas where I don't feel good
> about myself. I'd like for You to show me how much
> You love me. Help me remember that You look on my
> heart and not just what I look like outside. Help me
> reflect Your love to the people around me so they can
> see Your heart inside of me. In Jesus's name, amen.

As luck would have it, during the spring outdoor
band concert, the wind carried away Todd's sheet music
just as his trumpet solo was coming up.

# 6

## Extracurricular Activities
### What Do I Do After School?

Middle school is an excellent place to check out lots of stuff you may not have tried before, like sports, music groups, painting, or photography. We talked about electives in chapter 4, but there are a lot of cool after-school or extracurricular activities (stuff to do outside of school) you can check out now that you're at your new school. You might get involved in a sports team, a dance group, filmmaking, or a choir.

Not quite sure what activities you're interested in? Well, God created you with your own unique set of gifts, strengths, talents, and desires. So take this cool quiz to figure out some of your undiscovered talents and interests. Just put a check mark beside the items that describe you. If you're not sure but might want to check one of these out, put a question mark instead of a check mark. This little exercise might help you discover not only the things you're interested in but a little bit of who you are.

☐ I'd like to be in shows and plays. I'm creative and love being in front of a crowd. (If you checked this one, you should definitely look into the drama club and maybe even try out for the school play. You might be a star!)

☐ I like to dance and would enjoy getting better. (Did you check this? Then ask around about out your school's theater department. Or maybe your school has a dance or cheer team. If they don't, why not grab some tunes, find a teacher sponsor, and start one?)

☐ I'm really good at sports. Sometimes people call me a natural athlete. (If this is you, middle school will give you more opportunities to play sports like football, baseball, basketball, and volleyball. And in the spring, both boys and girls can go out for track too.)

☐ I love animals and would like to learn more about working with and caring for them. (If you checked this, find out if there's a 4-H club at your school or in your town. They do cool things like raise cows, pigs, and sheep. Or if you like

household pets, try volunteering at a local animal rescue shelter.)

☐ I'm a good student and would like to look into some advanced classes in math and science. (If science and math are your thing, check with your teacher to see what opportunities are available. They might know of some Math Olympics competitions you can join. Or you could start a science club, where you can perform crazy experiments in your secret basement laboratory and then be a star at the school science fair!)

☐ I'm a musician. I like playing the guitar or piano or drums or tuba or…(Middle school is a great way to rock your musical abilities. Find out if your school has a band or orchestra or a smaller jazz group. Maybe a teacher will even help you start a rock band!)

☐ I really like to sing, especially in a group. I have a good voice and would like to get better at reading music. (If you checked this one, then you definitely need to find out if your school has a choir. This is usually an actual class, so you'll go during the school day. But at some schools, choir is an extracurricular activity, so you might have practices before or after school. Either way, check it out. If you like singing, you'll love being in the school choir.)

## Checking In: *How to Make Good Decisions, Part 1*

*Trust in the LORD with all your heart, and lean not on your own understanding. In all your ways acknowledge Him, and He shall direct your paths.*

Proverbs 3:5-6 NKJV

Have you ever made a mistake? Done something dumb? Or wished you had a do-over? You're not alone.

In 1964, the Minnesota Vikings and the San Francisco 49ers played a nationally televised football game. When the 49ers fumbled the ball, Vikings defensive end Jim Marshall grabbed it and took off running. Unfortunately, he was running the wrong way! He made it all the way to the 49ers's end zone and ended up scoring a safety for San Francisco! Oops. Bet he wished he had a do-over on that one.

Have you ever felt like you've made a dumb decision? Or you ended up going the wrong way? Don't worry, everybody does dumb stuff. The good news is, if we ask God to forgive us, He will (1 John 1:9). So how do you learn to make good decisions? Whether you're deciding whether to try out for the soccer team or figuring out which friends to hang out with, here are two helpful ways to make good decisions. We'll look at more suggestions in chapter 9.

1. *Check out your Bible.* Will my Bible tell me whether I'm supposed to try out for volleyball or join the science fair? Probably not. But the Bible is full of God's wisdom we can apply to every part of our lives—friendships, getting along with parents, obedience, hard work, and being kind and honest. It's all in there.

2. *Try prayer.* So how do I pray? Does God really care if I take shop class or who I hang out with? Yep, He does. Psalm 139:2 says that He even knows our thoughts before we think them! So just talk with Him about how you're feeling. Prayer isn't about saying the right words; it's about being real with God. You might even say something like this: "God, it's been a rough day, but I'm glad You're in it with me."

**Extra Credit:** Read James 1:5-7 and see how God wants us to ask Him for wisdom.

Dear Lord, thank You for thinking about every detail of my life and caring for me. I know You let me make a lot of my own decisions, like which class I'm going to take and what sport I might try out for, but thanks for always guiding me when I come to You and ask. You're the best. Amen.

Sixth-grader Logan had no idea that so many eighth-graders were trying out for the team.

# 7

Important Things Every Kid Should Know About...

## Making the Team
### Tryouts, Auditions, and Elections

Now that you've taken the little quiz in chapter 6, you're ready to check out some of the new activities your school has to offer. Let's look at three extracurricular activities that almost every middle school makes available to its students: sports, performing arts, and student government. Who knows? You might end up getting involved in one or more of these!

### After-School Sports

One of the best ways to have fun, make friends, and keep active and healthy is to join a sports team. As you enter middle school, you'll discover a lot of new opportunities through the school or even through a community organization (like a park district or the YMCA) to play a sport that interests you.

You may have been playing a sport since you were little, or this might be a brand-new experience for you. Either way, just relax, have fun, and go for it! Find out if your school or organization has specific team tryouts. Then get in the habit of practicing on your own before the tryout day. Grab a friend or Mom or Dad, and catch, throw, run, spike, bat, shoot baskets, or whatever you need to do to get ready. Make sure you're eating right and getting plenty

Do you need to get a sports physical from your doctor before you can join the team? Make sure you schedule that in plenty of time for tryouts.

of sleep. You might also try running a little bit every day, especially if you've been a couch potato for a few months. Coaches tend to like their teams to be in good shape—go figure.

In addition to getting in shape, what can you do to stand out from the rest of the kids trying out for the team? Here are a few tips from our panel of experts that will help you get ready for tryouts and be a team player.

**1. Be prepared!** This sounds like the Boy Scout motto, but it works for team tryouts. Make sure you have whatever paperwork you need to try out for the team—insurance forms, permission slips, and stuff like that. And make sure you've got the right shoes, T-shirt, shorts, or whatever they want you to wear for the tryout.

**2. Be on time.** In fact, try to be a little bit early to the tryouts. You can't always control things like how fast you run or how far you can throw, but you can control things like being on time and prepared.

**3. Listen up.** Part of the fun of being on a team is playing around with your friends, but when the coach or an assistant is talking, it's time to zip it and listen. Show them respect. They tend to like that.

**4. Try your hardest.** Show up ready to work and to learn all you can from the coach and the other players. Stick around a little bit after the rest of the kids take off and practice the things that need work. You may not be the best athlete on the team, but you can be the hardest worker. And if you *are* the best athlete on the team *and* you work hard, the possibilities are endless!

If you do all these things and work hard, your tryouts should be a breeze. And most of all, have fun!

Now that you know what you should do to make the team, here's a list of the ways you can make sure you *don't* make the team.

## Top Ten Ways to Guarantee You *Won't* Make the Team

10. Show up to the tryouts wearing your Spider-Man pajamas.

9. Bring 50 people with you. Tell the coach they're your fan club.

8. When you're supposed to be doing drills, insist on taking selfies instead.

7. Answer everything the coach says with "That's what you think!"

6. Come wearing your helmet, pads, cleats, and team jersey...for swim practice.

5. Tell the coach that for today's drills, you've brought along your stunt double.

4. Inform the coach that you've developed some trick plays that involve you often running out of bounds and sometimes wearing the opponent's uniform.

3. During a scrimmage, insist on guarding the coach's three-year-old son.

2. When a teammate throws you the ball, stick your hands straight up in the air and shout "Eew, cooties!"

1. When the coach asks you why you didn't take a lap, say "Oh, I thought you said to take a *nap!*"

## Performing Arts: How to Nail the Audition

Middle school will also give you a chance to check out the performing arts—drama, band, choir, orchestra, and so on. If you've always thought being part of a production would be fun, go for it. You'll need to audition for most school productions and a few music groups. No sweat, you got this. Here are some helpful hints that will make your audition shine.

A lot of the tips for making a sports team fit with trying out for a play, musical, or orchestra (except maybe the running laps part). Here are just a few tips on auditioning for a part in the play that are sure to impress the director and score major points in the audition room.

**1. Come to the audition prepared.** Find out what the play is and read it if the scripts are available beforehand. Figure out which part you'd like to try out for. Does the part fit you? Read each scene your character is in a few times. Get a sense of what your character is like. Practice out loud with your mom or dad or a friend so you'll be more comfortable at the auditions.

**2. Get to the audition a few minutes early.** This will give you time to calm down and focus a little bit before you go in. By the way, if you're nervous about the audition, remember that everyone else is too. Besides, having a little nervous energy is a good thing. It helps your concentration and keeps you on your toes.

**3. Go for it!** When your name is called, take a deep breath, walk in, smile at the director, and go to the spot where they want you to stand.

**4. Follow directions.** Listen to the director and do what they suggest. This is key. They want to see if you're a good listener and if you can understand and take their direction. If they want you to be louder or softer, funnier or more serious, try to do it the way they want.

**5. Make it real.** If you're reading with another person in the scene, try not to be glued to your script. In other words, don't just look down and read like you're reciting a report at the front of the class. Relax and enjoy the moment. Look at and relate to the other actors whenever you can. Show the director you're a performer, not just a stilted reader.

**6. Sing your heart out!** If you're trying out for a musical and they want you to sing for the try out, choose a song that you feel comfortable with and memorize it. Bring the sheet music for the piano player to accompany you—you might be able to find it online.

> If you don't want to appear onstage for a show, there are a lot of fun things to do backstage—costumes, props, lighting, sound, even being the stage manager, which is pretty much everybody's boss. So check them out.

**7. Make a clean getaway.** When you're done, thank the director and get out of there. Don't ask when you'll hear about the parts or anything. They'll let you know when they'll make the casting announcements.

**8. Most of all, have fun!** This isn't brain surgery (unless you're trying out for *Frankenstein*). Being in a performance is a blast, so relax.

## Vote for Me! Politics and Your Middle School

Another cool way to get involved with your school (and meet some new people) is to run for a student office. Most middle schools have class and school officers and a student council that gets together regularly to improve stuff around the campus. Some of the officers get to plan fun events, like socials, dances, assemblies, and class competitions. Here's a short list of some of the main offices to consider running for.

## President

Obviously, this is the coolest office to hold. You get Secret Service protection, and you get to fly all over the world in your own private jet (kidding). If you're lucky, a kid named Jeffy will walk around with you wearing sunglasses and pretend to protect you.

As president, you run the student council meetings, give speeches, and sometimes represent the school at events with parents and community members. So you'll want to feel comfortable being around adults. Most school presidents start out in the student council or a lesser office to get to know their way around, and then they run for president later.

## Vice President

This is another important role in student government, although it comes with less pressure than being president. Of course, if the president is sick or gone, you'll take over and run the meetings in their absence. But you'll also get to talk with the president about important decisions and help out whenever possible. Definitely a cool position.

## Secretary

This person takes notes and/or records the student council meetings, so you probably want to be able to type or write fast. It also helps if you're a detail person. Once the meeting is finished, they'll probably have you type up the "minutes" (that's what they call what happened in the meeting) and send copies to everyone. You might also help with communication, letting the school know what's going on in the student government.

## Treasurer

This is the person who keeps track of the money. Most middle schools have a student fee that all the kids pay at the beginning of the year. It's usually between $5 and $20 per student, and it covers things like dances, materials for special projects, field days, holiday celebrations, and other stuff like that. Somebody's got to keep track of the cash, so that's where the treasurer comes in. It helps to be good at math and budgeting if you want this position, but you'll probably have a teacher around to help. So if you like keeping records and working with money, run for treasurer.

### Publicity Chair

This officer figures out cool ways to let the school know about upcoming events, like dances, sports, and assemblies. If you're creative and don't mind speaking in front of people, this might be a great position for you. It also helps if you're good at making posters and writing blurbs for the morning announcements. Or you might have some creative friends who can help you put together some amazing advertising for upcoming events.

### Student Council

This is a large group of kids who represent the entire school, usually by grade. So you might be a seventh-grade representative, or an eighth-grade representative, or whatever. Since you're the representative, kids might come up to you and say things like "This school needs a soda machine" or "How come we don't have a wrestling team?" or "Can you get Miss Stanford to stop giving us so much homework?" Then you take their ideas to the meeting and share them. (Probably not the last one.) Pretty cool. So running for student council is a great way to learn how student government works. Plus it's fun and interesting.

### Fun with Campaigning

To be involved in student government you need to get elected. Here are a few tips on running the best campaign you can.

1. Make sure kids know who you are. Try to meet lots of different kids from different groups. Make sure

they know your name. And when the
time comes, let them know you're
running for student office.

2. Gather some creative friends to come
up with a campaign slogan, some
posters, flyers, and maybe even a short
online video introducing yourself and
letting viewers know why they should
vote for you. Make all your materials
fun and catchy, but make sure they
include some real points so kids will
know you're serious about running for
office.

3. You'll probably have to give a speech
to the school to let them know why you deserve their vote. If
speaking in front of a group is a deal-breaker for you, you
can do one of two things: (1) shout "Forget about it!" at the
top of your lungs, run away, change your name, and move
to a foreign country, or (2) take a deep breath, remind yourself that almost everybody gets nervous before they speak, and
then go for it. Check out our sidebar below on speaking in
public. It's full of tips to help you make your speech fun, interesting, and memorable.

4. The important thing is to get your name out there so that on
election day, the other students will remember you and give
you their vote.

## Middle-School Social Life

Something that happens in middle school that you'll rarely find
in elementary school: social activities—dances, socials, class competitions, talent show...all kinds of opportunities to get involved
and have fun.

# How to Give a Speech

Are you giving a speech or presentation in front of your class? Here are a few good ideas that will help you knock it out of the park.

1. *Consider your audience.* If you're speaking to kids who you want to vote for you, make sure you connect well with them. Don't use big words that nobody ever uses in normal conversation. Include a little humor, but don't let it overshadow the points you're trying to make. Most of all, if you seem relaxed, your audience will be too.

2. *Don't wait until the last minute to write it.* Try to write your speech at least two days in advance. Write out your first draft, reread it to see if there are things you want to change, and then put it away for 24 hours. After that, look at it again. Chances are you'll see even more things you'll want to change to make it the best speech you can.

3. *Try not to read your speech word for word off your paper.* Write your main points on note cards to glance at during your speech. That way, you'll be able to look at the audience, and your eyes won't be glued to your paper. Try to make eye contact with some kids in the crowd, especially the ones who are smiling.

4. *Consider using visuals.* You might consider using either posters, PowerPoint slides, or other visual aids during your presentation. If people *see* things as well as hear them, they'll be more likely to enjoy your speech and remember what you said.

5. *Stay calm.* If you've got a little stage fright, take a long, slow, deep breath and remind yourself, "This is going to be a good thing and a great opportunity to succeed." You're going to be amazing!

## Dances/Socials

People started calling school dances "socials" years ago when nobody danced at middle-school dances. Back then, the music would play, and kids would see how close to the walls they could squeeze as they socialized, so the events were called "socials."

Even if you don't like to dance, socials are fun. You get to show up, listen to some music, talk to some of your friends, and enjoy some light refreshments. Think of it this way—it's way better than spending the afternoon in algebra class!

If your school socials are kind of lame, why not offer to help them make them better? Talk to whoever's in charge and suggest some games people can play, like a trivia contest, or some activities, like a photo booth with fun costumes or a game show with real prizes. Maybe a competition between different grades would add to the fun.

Oliver found that his creative interpretive dance at the school social didn't win him any friends.

*Talent Show*

Do you have a hidden talent? Can you do a great impression of a famous star? Can you sing? Can you do bird calls or imitate barnyard animals? Are you an amazing dancer? Comedian? Then check out the talent show. It will probably include auditions a few weeks before the performance, so make sure you practice so you'll be ready. This is your chance to show off your skills!

Try not to do a lip sync act unless you have some impressive choreography to go with it. And here are a few other ideas you might consider not doing.

1. Do vocal impressions of famous presidents, including Washington, Jefferson, and Rutherford B. Hayes. Make sure they've all been dead for at least 100 years. That way nobody really knows what they sounded like.

2. Ad-lib an entire Italian opera while somebody hits you in the face with a whipped-cream pie.

3. Play the piano by hitting your head on the keys. Tell the audience you're playing by ear.

4. Sing a duet with your performing goldfish.

5. Juggle flaming bagels.

## What If It Doesn't Go Well?

Sometimes things don't work out the way you hoped they would. After a disappointment, like usually maybe a day or two later, you won't feel quite so upset about things. So after your emotions have settled down, take some time to think through what happened. Is there something you could have done better, like practice or be more prepared? Or was it something completely out of your control—like the need for someone taller for the play? Or you were 60 pounds too light for the offensive line? Either way, hang in there. See what you can do next time that will increase your chances of success.

---

Checking In: *Disappointments—Been There, Done That*

---

*[Jesus] understands our weaknesses since he had the same temptations we do, though he never once gave way to them and sinned.*

Hebrews 4:15

Nobody likes to be left out or feel rejected, so if you didn't make the team or the play, take some time to let yourself feel upset or sad about it. Nobody succeeds all the time (even though it seems like some kids do). If you're feeling sad, upset, or angry, that's okay. That's natural.

And believe it or not, God understands what you're going through. "What?" you exclaim. "How can that be? He's God! He doesn't know what it's like to get rejected or turned down? He can do anything He wants!"

But God *does* know what it's like to feel rejected and betrayed. Remember what happened to Jesus? His enemies arrested Him, His friends deserted Him, and one of His best buds, Peter, denied even knowing Him. The Scripture above says that Jesus understands everything we go through because He's been through it too. So what do we do?

When you're experiencing disappointment, go to Him. Be honest and let Him know how you're feeling. Psalm 62:8 says, "Trust in him at all times you people; pour out your hearts to him" (NIV). So go ahead, be honest, and tell Him everything, even if you're feeling a little mad at Him. Let Him come near to you and help you feel better. Even though you've just been disappointed, remember He loves you so much, He'd even die for you. As a matter of fact, He did so that He could be friends with you. Remember that He knows all about disappointment and even heartache—He's been there.

**Extra Credit:** Read Isaiah 53:3 and Matthew 26:69-75.

> Dear Lord, I guess You know what I'm feeling right now, and I thank You for that. Sometimes when I'm disappointed, I don't want to come to You. But help me think of You first when I go through hard stuff. Help me learn from my disappointments and get ready for the next challenge I might face. Thanks for loving me no matter what and for understanding me. In Jesus's name, amen.

Do you have much homework tonight, Mason?

# 8

## Homework
### The Good, the Bad, and the Ugly

Once you get to middle school, you'll notice you have more homework than you had in elementary school. Reading, math, book reports, group projects...it's almost like each teacher forgets you have other classes to study for!

Homework can be hard, but there are a few things you can do to make sure you get all your assignments done and still have time for important stuff like basketball, pizza, music, and binge-watching your favorite TV shows.

**1. Organize.** If you need your French book for your French class, remember to take it with you every time. As you get a little older, you'll notice your teachers will start trusting you to take care of things more, and they'll begin to treat you more like an adult (though they probably won't let you borrow their car anytime soon). So make sure you're organized with your books and materials. Don't be one of those people who always borrow paper or pencils. That gets old fast. Make sure you bring your own supplies.

**2. Don't put stuff off.** This is probably the most important thing you'll learn in middle school. Keep on top of your classes. Once you fall way behind in your assignments, it feels impossible to ever catch

up. Learn to take notes during class. When the teacher's talking about stuff, try jotting down the most important things. You'll need this skill a lot when you get to high school. Of course, you don't have to take down every word, just the important stuff.

**3. Organize your study area.** Do you like to study sitting at a desk? At the kitchen table? On your bed? It doesn't matter where you study, but find a place that's comfortable and that doesn't have a lot of distractions. Probably in the middle of the family room while your little sister has her play pals over is not optimal. And wherever you end up studying, make sure the light is good so you can see your papers and stuff.

**4. Have everything you need right at hand.** That means where you can reach it. Do you need a computer for what you're about to do? Paper? Pens and pencils? Your books? Gather everything and have them together. That way you won't waste time searching for the supplies you need to finish your math, English, or science.

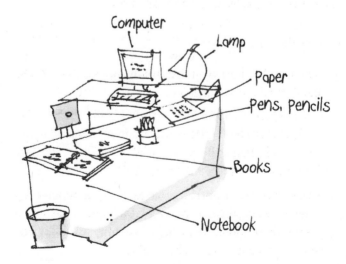

**5. If you're having trouble understanding the subject, ask for help!** It's no big deal. Talk to your teacher. Or get one of your parents to help you. You might do well with having an older kid come and tutor you. Totally worth it—you'll feel much better and get a lot more done. Sometimes it's hard to ask for help, but it sure beats sitting there in class lost and feeling like they're speaking fourteenth-century Portuguese the whole time.

**6. Manage distractions.** If part of your homework involves using a computer, here's a tip on not getting caught up by various distractions, like Facebook, Instagram, kitty videos, and games that are calling your name from their secret hiding place in cyberspace. Be honest and admit that these things can easily lead you away from the task at hand—your homework. If this is becoming a problem, set a time limit for the fun stuff. Say, "Okay, I'm going to allow myself to check Facebook or play a game for 15 minutes or a half hour. Then I'll work on my homework." Or you could work on your homework for a half an hour and then reward yourself by playing a game for 20 minutes. Just don't get lured into the internet vortex, or you'll never get anything done at all!

## Learning Styles: Which One Are You?

How do you learn? There are basically three ways that kids (and adults) gather information:

1. *Hands-on.* You learn by doing. You work well with your hands, and if you do something once, you've usually got it.

2. *Listen up!* You can learn and remember stuff just by hearing it. This helps when you're in the classroom listening to the teacher talk about different subjects. Most people don't learn this way, so if you don't, not to worry.

3. *Well, look at that.* If you're a visual learner, you remember things by seeing them. A video, a PowerPoint presentation, posters, illustrations...these help you learn and remember stuff. You might also learn by reading.

When you figure out what kind of learner you are, try to study in that way. If it helps you to write or draw something about the information (hands-on), then do it! If you're more of a "listen up" learner, you might have your mom or dad read some of the material out loud to you so you'll remember it. And if you're a visual learner, see if reading works for you. Go online and find information about the subject (just make sure it's accurate). YouTube might even have some videos about what you're studying. Those are good ways for a visual learner to study.

## When Is the Best Time for You to Study?

Before you dive into studying at home, the best thing to do is figure out what kind of homework person you are. Do you like to come home and start on it right away? Or do you wait until the last minute to get stuff done? Or are you somewhere in the middle? Here's another nonscientific quiz for you to take to see what kind of studier you are. Check the item below that best describes you and your homework habits:

☐ I like to come home and get right at it. I can't unwind or play if I have something hanging over my head, like a reading assignment or building a volcano with vinegar and baking soda. So I get my assignments done as soon as I can. Then I can relax.

☐ I like to ease into my homework. I might come home, play with the dog (or cat or gerbil) for a while, maybe get something to eat, watch a little TV, and then get to my homework. After all, I've been using my brain all day in class—it needs a break!

☐ Honestly, I'm a procrastinator. I leave everything until the last minute, and then I try to get it all done in the shortest amount of time possible. After all, I work best under pressure.

☐ To be brutally honest (don't tell anyone), I don't do my homework at all. I know it'll probably get me in trouble with my teachers and parents, but I don't care. To me, homework seems kind of pointless.

Thanks for your honesty. Now you know how you're going to approach doing your schoolwork every day. You might want to relax a little bit before you start or jump right into it—do it the way that works best for you. If you checked the fourth option (you really hate schoolwork and usually don't do it), check out the sidebar below.

## It All Seems Pointless

*"I just don't care. Homework—in fact, school for that matter—seems totally pointless. I'd rather just sleep in, hang out with my friends, and play video games. Does that make me a bad person?"*

No, not at all. A lot of kids go through a time when they question the point of school, friends, and even what life is about. If you feel this way for a few days or a week, it's not a big deal. But if this sounds like you all the time, there's probably something else going on too. And it may have nothing at all to do with school. Is there something going on at home that is bugging you? Are your parents not getting along, or did they divorce a while back? Are you having fights with your brothers and sisters? Are you feeling lonely or hopeless?

Sometimes videos games, sleeping, or binge-watching TV are ways to escape from life. If you're feeling this way a lot, find somebody to tell about it. If you can't talk to your mom or dad, then try talking to a teacher, a coach, a youth pastor, or some other adult you trust and respect. It's not always going to be this way, and there are some things you can do to get back to where you want to be. Talking to someone might be the first step.

## Raising Your Parents: Homework

You might talk with your parents about your homework style and even show them this quiz. That way they'll know what to expect from you in the homework department. If you like to jump right into it, tell them. Or if you need to relax a little before you start your homework, share that too. If they know what to expect from you, you might have a lot less conflict about your study habits.

## Vocabulary Words Kids Need to Know

Get ready, because in middle school you're going to see an upgrade in vocabulary—you know, the words people use and expect you to understand. So why not get a jump on things and start to learn some of these new words right now? Here are some that you'll need to know before you get to the seventh grade. Check them out. If you don't know their definition, look them up online or in a dictionary:

| | | | | |
|---|---|---|---|---|
| abdicate | bewilder | eligible | mandatory | resolve |
| abruptly | bias | estimate | narrate | signify |
| acknowledge | cause | impartial | necessity | suspense |
| acquire | compel | indifferent | omit | tentative |
| allege | contrast | industrious | opposition | toxic |
| antagonize | deceitful | inevitable | persuasive | treason |
| authentic | demeanor | legendary | quote | viewpoint |

## Now What?

Okay, so you've organized your work space; you've got your number 2 pencils, paper, and books close at hand; you've given yourself 20 minutes to play a game online; and you've even gotten help with your hardest subjects. But what if you *still* haven't done your homework? Here are ten excuses you can try on your teacher for not finishing it. (Let us know how it goes.)

# Top Ten Excuses for Not Having Your Homework Done

10. Aliens hovered over my house and beamed up all my homework. They said they needed this kind of brilliance in their own galaxy.

9. I had just finished my homework when two Russian spies switched my briefcase at the drop-off point.

8. A plague of locusts swarmed my bedroom, devouring everything in their path, which, alas, included my homework.

7. I misunderstood the assignment and answered all the homework questions in Mandarin.

6. I think I caught a virus from my computer.

5. I hated the idea of clear-cutting an entire forest just so I could write my homework on a piece of paper, so I skipped it.

4. An angry flock of chickens stormed my room and pecked at my homework paper until it was unrecognizable.

3. A Hollywood producer called and said he wanted to make a movie out of my life. But it was running long, so we had to cut out all the homework parts.

2. The dog did my homework, and I ate it. The homework, not the dog.

1. You gave us homework?

## Glasses: Fashion Statement or Middle School Necessity?

If you have trouble seeing the board or even the teacher, go get your eyes checked. You might need glasses to improve your vision. And who knows? Your glasses may make you look cooler and more intelligent. Or just ask to sit a little closer to the front of the class. If you're falling behind in class and your grades are starting to slip, it might be because you can't see the stuff very well.

## How to Ace a Test

Once you get into sixth grade, there will be a lot more tests and quizzes you'll need to study for. No big deal—it's all part of middle school. There are two ways you get information for tests: (1) from the teachers' lectures during class and (2) from the textbook chapters you read as part of your homework. If you do these two things, keep up with your assignments, ask questions, and let your teachers know when you're having problems, chances are good you'll do well on the tests. Review your class notes before each test, and check out the parts of the book your teacher said were important.

About a week before your test, study a little bit each night. But try using *different* ways of studying. One night, write down the information on flash cards and practice with them. The next night, find the key words you need to remember and write them down. The night after that, if you feel like you know the material, try *teaching* it to your mom or dad. If you can teach it, you really know the information.

Now that you've studied in different ways and listened in class, the day of the test is here. No sweat. You got this. Here are a couple things to remember when you're taking the test:

1. Read the directions twice. You sure don't want to misunderstand them and get wrong answers.

2. Answer the easy questions first. That saves time and gives you a boost of confidence.

3. When you're done, before you turn in the test, double check your answers. Make sure you said what you meant to say.

And there you have it. Tests? No problem.

## What to Eat Before a Test

On the day of a big test (or even a little quiz), consider eating some of these foods for breakfast:

1. *Oatmeal.* Oatmeal has a bunch of nutrients (like manganese and selenium) that help keep your brain healthy.

2. *Eggs.* Have a scrambled or fried egg the morning of your test. Eggs are rich in protein, which helps create amino acids that form neurotransmitters in your brain, helping you think more clearly. Who knew?

3. *Water.* Make sure you're well hydrated before a test—and not with soft drinks or even energy drinks. Too much sugar might make you all buzzy and then sleepy, which is not a good

combination when you're trying to remember the names of all of Henry the Eighth's wives.* Just stick with water.

4. *Nuts.* If your teacher doesn't mind, take along a baggie filled with almonds, walnuts, hazelnuts, or cashews to the test with you. They're full of omega-3 fatty acids, which are good for learning, memory, and concentration.

## Checking In: *Working Hard or Hardly Working?*

*All hard work brings a profit.*

Proverbs 14:23 NIV

It might be hard to believe right now, but God has great plans for you. You might end up as a space shuttle commander, an NBA superstar, a television writer, a missionary, a comic-book illustrator, a teacher, or a restaurant owner. God knows your talents, desires, and gifts, and He would like nothing more than for you to succeed at what He has planned for you.

Right now, you're in training. You might be asking, "But what does algebra have to do with me being the next LeBron James?" or "How is world history going to help me be a music star?" Believe it or not, going to school will help you get ready for the next big thing God has planned for you. And you want to be ready, don't you?

Right now, your life assignment is—are you ready for this?—to go to school. And if you're going to be an NBA star or musical sensation, you can practice that stuff in your free time. The Bible says in Proverbs 14:23 that in *all* work (that means even algebra), there is profit. It *will* pay off. So do your best on your homework, your sports practices, your music rehearsals, and everything else you're

---

* Catherine of Aragon, Anne Boleyn, Jane Seymour, Anne of Cleves, Catherine Howard, and Catherine Parr.

doing right now. And remember—every day you're getting closer to your goal. Cool, huh?

**Extra Credit:** Read Jeremiah 29:11, and see how God feels about you, His plans for you, and your future.

> Dear Lord, sometimes it's hard for me to see the importance of doing some of these classes. But help me see that You want me to work hard, do my best, and get something out of all my studies—even if it's just learning to hang in there and not give up. Thanks. In Jesus's name, amen.

Being the youngest of four kids, Noah found that "back-to-school shopping" meant looking through his brothers' hand-me-downs.

# *9*

## Being Stuck in the Middle
### Not a Kid but Not Grown Up

Sixth, seventh, and eighth grades are kind of awkward years for almost everybody. Oh, sure, you're going to have some great times and create some amazing memories, but there might be some awkward moments too. Some kids might look like they're breezing through this tumultuous time, but trust us—everybody is feeling a little bit uncomfortable.

For one thing, you're not a little kid anymore, but you're not an adult either. You still need your mom and dad for things like getting around and buying stuff. But at the same time, you're not their little boy or girl anymore either (even though you still like to sneak in and play with your toys from before when no one's around).

Here's the thing—you're entering a period of your life called "adolescence." You've heard that word before, and in chapter 11, we'll talk about what adolescence is (and even more important, what it *isn't*). Meanwhile, what do you do in this in-between time? Glad you asked.

### Responsibility: I'm Not Sure I'm Ready!

Part of the middle-school experience is making good choices and gaining more and more responsibility. "Yikes," you say, "I'm not sure if I'm ready to take a lot of responsibility! I'm still just a kid!" Don't worry, your parents and you can decide just what kind of things you can be responsible for. Paying the family bills? Hiring a contractor to do a nice family room addition on your house? Handling your family's dental hygiene? Not so much. But can you take over the care of the family pet—feeding them, making sure they have water, and taking them for walks? Yeah, you could do that. How about taking out the trash? Getting yourself up for school and turning in your assignments on time? Yeah, you can do that. See? Responsibility isn't that hard. In fact, most of the time, you'll feel great when you've accomplished something, especially if it's a little bit challenging.

## Ten Things Every Middle Schooler Should Know How to Do

As you turn 12 or 13, you'll start to explore areas in your life where you can become more independent—where you don't need Mom and Dad to do everything for you. So here's a list of ten things you might try to learn how to do before you leave middle school.

### 1. Make a Few Meals

One of the best and easiest ways to start feeling more independent is to learn how to cook. We're not talking a ten-course meal, but how about something easy, like scrambled eggs, bacon, and toast? Or grilled cheese sandwiches and tomato soup? Chicken and rice? Easy. Check out Pinterest for some easy to follow recipes you can make. Check with your mom or dad to see if you have all the ingredients. Then just follow the directions, and soon, with a little practice, you'll be a regular master chef!

And don't forget, cleaning up the kitchen afterward is part of preparing the meal!

### 2. Entertain Yourself Without a Screen

What does that mean? Try drawing stuff in a sketchbook, reading a book, shooting some baskets, making up a story, or coming up with some fun ideas to do with your younger brothers or sisters. All without your phone, laptop, or tablet. When was the last time you spent a half hour just dreaming about stuff, like what you would do if someone gave you $10 million? Or if you could do anything in the whole world, what would it be? Or if you could have a superpower, what would it be? (Ours would be to fly like Iron Man.)

### 3. Shop for Food

This is an important thing to know how to do. Make a list, figure out about how much everything is going to cost, and go to the store and buy the stuff (probably with your parents' money). After a while, you'll figure out the best prices and how to save some cash while you're there.

### 4. Keep a Calendar

Keeping track of your own schedule is one of the cool things about growing up. You can show your parents that you can be responsible. Do you have soccer practice on Wednesday? Write it down or put it in your phone. How about a test this Friday in history? Make sure you've got that too. And hey, you might even try studying for it. See how easy keeping a calendar can be?

### 5. Use Good Manners

This is an important skill to develop now and for the future. Practice looking people in the eye, smiling, and speaking up when you talk. If you're a guy, hold the door open for girls and older people. Shake hands. Don't interrupt when other people are talking. Practice listening. People love that.

### 6. Do Chores on Your Own

You should learn not only how to do some chores, like loading the dishwasher right and mowing the lawn, but also how to keep track of them yourself. When you're grown up and out living on your own, guess what? Your mom isn't going to be there to remind you to take out the trash. Ooh, stinky. You might set a reminder to feed the dog, mow the lawn, or rake the leaves. Learn how to do it now, and you'll be glad later.

### 7. Swim

If you don't know how to swim or don't feel comfortable in the water, sign up for some swim lessons. Check out your local YMCA or park district or community center. Chances are that in a couple of lessons, you'll know all the basics of swimming. That way you'll feel secure and confident around the pool. Cannonball!

### 8. Manage Money

This is something that a lot of adults still don't get. If you have a part-time job or get an allowance, try this idea. Get three jars.

- One is for *saving* money for a big purchase (an Xbox or a bike), a vacation or mission trip, or maybe even college.

- The next jar contains money for *spending*. That's the fun one—money for movies, snacks, music, the latest book or game...whatever. It's for stuff you want right away.

- The third jar is money for *sharing*. The Bible tells us that we should be giving away at least 10 percent of our money to help other people. After all, when you think about it, everything we own comes from God, and giving is a good reminder of that. You can give to your church or a charity. Have you heard about an organization that helps kids? Or a group that helps people in Africa have access to clean water? Try giving them some money each time you get paid. It'll feel good, you'll be obeying God, and you'll be helping people.

So here's how this jar thing works. Let's say you receive ten dollars. You put one (10 percent) into sharing, four into savings, and five into spending. That's a good habit to develop. Try it for a while.

### 9. Manage Yourself

This goes along with the calendar thing, but as you get a little older, try depending on your mom or dad less to get you up for school, help you get ready, pick up your room, and stuff like that. Doing more for yourself will start to feel good as you look at everything you're accomplishing.

### 10. Develop Personal Hygiene

What does that mean? Simply put, it means *don't stink*! Take a shower at least every other day. Brush your teeth and keep your hair clean. Trust us—people will like you a whole lot better that way. And as you enter this new stage in life, you might find that you need to start wearing deodorant. Just slap a little on under both arms before you go out, and you'll smell a lot better. See chapter 11 for some helpful tips on personal hygiene.

And if you're a guy who loves to wear the same pants and shirt most of the time, you might try wearing clean clothes once in a while. We all know you love that T-shirt from camp two summers ago, but when you wear it 20 days in a row, people will be able to smell you coming blocks away. Try to wear clean clothes every day.

So there you have it. If you can do these ten things by the time you get out of eighth grade, you'll be on your way to a happy, independent life. Good job!

## Raising Your Parents: Earning Trust

Here's a little secret about parents. When you start to show them you're becoming more responsible—doing things like cleaning your room without being told, putting out the trash, doing your homework, getting up and getting to school on time—they'll start to notice and begin to trust you more and give you a little more freedom. If they can trust you in the small things, they might just start trusting you with more and more. Just a thought.

And if they don't notice all the good stuff you're doing, you could say something like, "Have you noticed that I've been getting up and getting ready for school without you nagging me lately? Well, I think it's time for me to have a little more freedom. How about a nice condo in Hawaii?" Or maybe something a little more realistic.

---

## Checking In: *How to Make Good Decisions, Part 2*

*In everything you do, put God first, and He will direct you and crown your efforts with success.*
Proverbs 3:6

We've already looked at a couple of ways to make good choices in chapter 6: (1) check out your Bible for direction, and (2) ask God to help through prayer. Here are three more ideas to help you be smart and make good decisions:

*1. Get some help.* If you're stuck on making a decision, like who to hang out with or what sport to try out for, talk to somebody about it. Probably somebody a little older than you because your friends are basically in the same place you are, trying to figure things out for themselves. So talk to your mom or dad, a grandparent, an older brother or sister, your youth pastor, a teacher or coach, or a good friend. Sometimes getting a second opinion will help you see things more clearly.

*2. Pay attention to your desires.* God gives us passions for certain things. Are you an artist? That's a gift God gave you, so He wants you to use and enjoy it. Are you good at sports, music, or making people laugh? God wants us to enjoy life and do the things He's created us to do. Sometimes God uses our good desires to direct us.

*3. How are things working out?* Sometimes you can watch how circumstances work out and see how God is directing your path. If you made the football team, it might indicate that God wants you to do that right now. Or if you were chosen to be the news editor out of 20 other kids, God may have the school newspaper in His plans for you. Watch carefully how things work out. Sometimes God will direct you through circumstances.

The good news is that as you grow and practice these things, making smart decisions will start to get a lot easier.

**Extra Credit:** Are you trying to decide right now? Use one or more of the ideas we've shared with you—check out your Bible, ask God to direct you, find someone to give you advice, check your desires, and watch how things work out. These are some great ways to start!

> Dear Lord, sometimes it's hard for me to figure out what
> I'm supposed to do and which way I'm supposed to go.
> Some of my decisions are easy—don't rob banks or take
> candy away from little kids—but a lot of my choices aren't
> always that clear. Will You help me do the right thing as
> I go through life in middle school? Thanks a lot. Amen.

Sarah never realized she had so many friends
until she wanted to take a selfie.

# 10

## Making Friends
### How to Do It

One of the cool things about middle school is meeting a bunch of new people as you participate in classes, activities, sports, and clubs. Most public middle schools receive students from several elementary schools, so chances are you're going to end up hanging out with kids you didn't know last year.

"But how do I make friends? I'm just a dorky sixth (or seventh or eighth) grader!" You might be a little quiet, and making friends might be hard for you. But never fear—we've got some helpful hints to make the whole thing easier and a whole lot more fun!

### Tips for Making Friends

**1. Be a good listener.** When you're around a new person, ask some questions. "When did you start playing basketball?" "How did you get to be so good at the guitar?" "Do you have any brothers or sisters? Do they drive you crazy?" Here's a little secret: People like to talk about themselves and their experiences. If you're a good listener, kids will like to be around you.

But make sure you get a chance to talk a little bit too. Having a one-sided friendship where the other person does all the talking for

months at a time isn't a very good friendship. You deserve to be listened to too.

**2. Get involved.** This is a great way to meet new people. Find a group or club that interests you. Sometimes just doing things and spending time around other kids will help you start and build friendships. It might be hard to go by yourself to the first club or team meeting, but get courageous and go for it. Remember, some of the other kids might be a little nervous too. Who knows? Maybe you'll be the one who makes another kid feel comfortable.

**3. Introduce yourself.** When you see a potential friend, go ahead and reach out. It sounds scary, but it's so worth it. You could start by just going over to the person and introducing yourself: "Hi, my name is _____." Or start by offering a short compliment: "Cool shirt" (or shoes or backpack). Or start by asking a question: "Do you know who that teacher is?"

**4. Be yourself.** Don't try to be somebody else. Just let your own awesome personality shine through. People can spot when you're not being real. Just be yourself. And if you find yourself needing to act like someone else to try to join a group, chances are that's not the group for you.

**5. Be kind.** Treat people the way you'd like to be treated. Don't make fun of them. Don't talk behind their backs. Be real. Be honest. Other kids like that.

**6. Be loyal.** If someone else is putting down or badmouthing your friend, stand up and say something like "That's not true. Alex (or Jennifer or Chloe) is cool. You just have to get to know them." Friendships that are loyal are the ones that last.

So now that you know what to do to make some good friends, here are some ideas of how *not* to treat a friend.

### Five Ways to Wreck a Perfectly Good Friendship

1. Soak your friend head to toe with a fire hose seconds before they have their school picture taken.

2. When they tell you something in secret, rent a billboard across the street and share it with entire school.

3. When you're having a conversation, see if you can speak for 45 minutes straight without pausing to take a breath or ask anything about them.

4. Do the "spoiler alert" thing and tell them the end of a movie they're about to go see.

5. Try to think only of yourself 24/7, 365 days a year.

## Frenemies

As you enter middle school, you might find that there's a lot of drama between friends. You might be best friends with someone on Monday, but by Tuesday, they're your worst enemy. Someone will be talking behind someone else's back, they won't get invited to a party, or they break up with their girlfriend or boyfriend—and then people around them start to take sides, and the whole thing turns into an unhappy, emotional mess. It's called *drama*, and most middle school kids are familiar with it. Why is this happening? And why now?

One of the reasons has to do with the stuff going on in a middle schooler's body and brain. One of the things you'll experience at this age is a strong surge of emotions—and sometimes for no reason whatsoever! We'll talk more about that in a little bit.

So what do you do when your friends start acting weird and overly dramatic? Well, it might be good to step back a little and maybe even to spend some time with a few other friends until the drama settles down a little bit. Sometimes a little time away is just the right thing. You could say something like "I'm sorry that happened. Hope you guys are able to work it out." Sometimes that's all it takes to calm someone down and lower the drama meter just a little bit.

One more thing. If you find yourself in a group where one or two of the kids have a lot more power than everybody else—they set the rules, they choose what you talk about, they choose who's "in"

## Helpful Tip: Join a Youth Group

Another way to meet people is through a church youth group. If you already go to church with your family, ask around and see if they have a middle school group. Sometimes they'll meet with the high school group. Youth groups usually meet on Sunday mornings or Sunday nights or Wednesday nights. If you don't already attend a church, check with some of your friends and see if they know about a cool youth group in your town. Check it out. It's a good way to have a lot of fun, meet people, get some good direction, and learn more about God.

and who's "out"—you might want to choose another group. Those kinds of groups usually end badly. So exit quietly and find some better friends as soon as you can.

## Checking In: *Walk Across the Room*

*A man who has friends must himself be friendly.*
Proverbs 18:24 NKJV

Most of us don't think about friends and relationships that much. We figure they're just there. But did you know that God designed us to be in relationships? We're not supposed to be isolated from one another. Way back in the beginning, right after He created Adam, God said, "It is not good for the man to be alone." The same is true for you, so it's natural for you to want to be around your friends. Even if you're an introvert, it's not good for you to be alone all the time. Ask God to direct you to some cool kids who love God and will love you. He'll do it because He doesn't want you to be alone. Meeting somebody new might be a little risky—you might have to take the first step, but go ahead and reach out. Walk across the room and meet someone new. It'll be totally worth it.

**Extra Credit:** Decide to meet someone new this week—someone in class or on your team or at your youth group. Follow some of the suggestions above and see how it goes.

Dear Lord, thank You for creating me to have friends
and have people around me, people to talk to when
I'm doing great or when things aren't going so well.
Please lead me to a couple of good friends who will be
there for me. And help me be the kind of friend who's
always there for them too. In Jesus's name, amen.

Adolescence Fact #387: Sometimes girls grow a
lot faster than boys.

# 11

## Adolescence
### Facial Hair, Greasy Skin, and Zits

Adolescence. You may have had a class to help you understand what it is or even seen one of those videos about boys and girls and your changing body and all that jazz. Well, like it or not, either you're about to enter adolescence or you're right in the middle of this stage of your life. During this time, you might hit a giant growth spurt—or not. You might be the biggest kid in your class or the smallest. If you're a guy, your voice might be changing and cracking, sometimes in the most embarrassing situations. You're probably getting hair in new places and sweating a lot more, and you might even have some zit problems. All in all, sounds great, doesn't it?

What is this adolescence deal, anyway? The short answer is that it's your body and your brain getting ready for adulthood. "What? You mean like getting married, landing a job, buying a house, paying taxes, and figuring out my retirement? I'm only 12 years old! I'm not ready for adulthood!"

No, that's not exactly what we're talking about. Adolescence is just a natural way for you to begin to grow up physically, emotionally, and mentally. It's totally natural even though there may be times when it doesn't feel that way. Adolescence, as awkward as it might be sometimes, is a good thing. Your body is just getting ready to turn into a healthy adult body. And don't worry; these changes won't happen all at once. Most of the time they'll be so gradual, you won't even notice them. Let's look at some of the things you might expect during this time.

## Physical Changes: For Guys Only

Here are five things you might notice starting to happen.

**1. Growth spurts.** You may have already hit a growth spurt, although usually this happens around age 13 or 14. You might grow as much as ten inches in a year! And you might notice your muscles getting bigger and stronger, especially if you're exercising and/or playing a sport. Your coordination might not keep up with your physical growth, so don't be surprised if you seem a little clumsier and less coordinated than you were just a few months ago. This is normal, and you'll get over it soon. If you think you're too skinny, don't worry—if you keep active, you'll fill out later, when you're 17 or 18 or 19. See chapter 5 for some tips on exercising.

**2. Squeak.** Your voice will start changing around this time too, so don't be surprised if it kind of squeaks and cracks sometimes. It'll feel like you're going from high to low and then back again—sometimes in the same sentence! Don't worry; you're just developing a cool, adult guy voice. Who knows? You might end up sounding like that guy who announces all the movie trailers. "In a world where..."

**3. Hair.** Adolescence is the time you'll start to get hair in new places on your body. Like under your arms and down in your private parts. No big deal, it just means you're growing up.

**4. Skin.** As you reach this age, your sweat- and oil-producing glands get more active. When they get clogged, you might experience some skin problems. Your changing hormones and stress level can also cause acne (the scientific term is "zits"). Check out the skin tips below for some good ideas on how to keep your face clear.

**5. Close shave.** At some point, you'll start getting some cool facial hair and need to shave. Probably when you're 13 or 14. At first, it will look like a little fuzz on your lip or chin (it does on almost every guy), but after a while, it will start to grow in. At first, you might need to shave once or twice a week, but unless you want to start growing a beard, it'll soon be every day. It's not that hard—just have your dad show you how or go online. There are "how-to" videos that show you how to shave without nicking up your face. Ooh, smooth.

### Hygiene and Grooming: Don't Stink

Here's a thought. As you enter adolescence, you're going to start sweating more than you used to. That means you've got to work harder at not stinking. It's not that hard—just shower as often as you need to. That will probably mean at least every other day. And

don't just rinse off. Scrub under your arms and in your groin area with soap or body wash. Maybe even wash your hair occasionally. Then after you towel off, slap on a little deodorant. Quick, easy, and you won't lose any friends.

## Physical Changes: For Girls Only

Here are five things you can expect when you hit this amazing stage in your life.

**1. Growth spurt.** You might be experiencing a growth spurt. It's not at all unusual for girls to be taller than boys in sixth and seventh grade. And then when eighth and ninth grade rolls around, the boys usually catch up. You might be a little physically awkward and clumsy for a while, but soon your coordination will catch up with your body.

**2. You'll get rounder.** One of the first things you'll notice as you reach puberty is you'll start filling out. You might have been skinny before, but now your hips and breasts are starting to develop. Some girls will develop right away, while some others will take longer. There's nothing wrong—everyone grows at a different pace.

**3. Hair everywhere!** Another result of puberty is that you'll start to grow hair in new places, like under your arms and in your private parts. It's perfectly natural, so don't be surprised when it starts to appear. Your arm and leg hair will start to appear too. Usually around 13 or 14, girls start shaving their legs. So if you don't like the hair, you might consider that. Have your mom or an older sister show you how to do that.

**4. Skin.** Just like the boys (we know you read their section, admit it) your skin is going to be a little oilier. You'll need to take a little more time caring for your face. Below are some ideas on how to keep that beautiful face of yours glowing.

**5. Periods will start.** This is when the lining of the uterus (womb) is shed every month. You'll experience bleeding and maybe some pain before and during your period, like headaches or stomach cramps. These can be unpleasant, but they're normal. If you have any concerns about your period, talk to your mom or doctor.

## The Dreaded Zit Attack!

It's not an attack, and you don't have to dread it. It just sounds more dramatic when we say it that way. As you enter adolescence, you'll discover a little excess oil in your hair and on your skin. Make sure you keep your hair nice and clean by showering and washing it at least every other day. And if you've got a zit problem, not to worry, here are some hints to get rid of them and keep your skin looking great.

## Skin Care Tips

Wash your face twice a day—maybe once in the morning and once in the evening before bed. Use warm water and a good gentle soap. Washing twice a day keeps your face clean, keeps the oils down, and gets rid of the yucky stuff that can cause some blemishes.

As tempting as it is, don't pop your zits. This pushes infected material down into your skin and can cause problems later. Gross! And try not to pick at them. This could lead to scarring on your face, and nobody wants that.

Wash your hands often. You probably don't even know it, but you touch your face about a thousand times a day, and all the stuff that you've touched can get all over your face. So keep your hands clean too.

Drink lots of water. Keeping your body hydrated keeps you healthy and can also help flush junk from your system. And when your system is clean everything runs better. That includes your skin.

If you've got some stubborn skin problems and need some help, you might try using a cleanser containing time-released benzoyl peroxide. That will help get rid of zits and clear up your face. Have your

mom check with your doctor or pharmacist to see if this might be helpful for you.

## Catch Some Zzzs

Don't be surprised if when you enter sixth or seventh grade, you have more trouble waking up in the morning. Adolescents (that's you) tend to need more sleep than little kids and adults. It's part of the growing process. You might be tempted to stay up later studying or watching TV, but whenever you can, try to get at least seven hours of sleep a night. If you can do it, get eight or nine hours. That's even better. That way you're not falling asleep while your biology teacher is explaining the inner workings of a frog. Some middle schools are beginning to start their days a little later to help kids get more sleep. You might suggest that to one of those nice people who work in the office.

### Checking In: *Pretty Simple*

*Love the Lord your God with all your heart and with all your soul and with all your mind." This is the first and greatest commandment. And the second is like it: "Love your neighbor as yourself.*
Matthew 22:37-39 NIV

As you grow in your friendship with Jesus, you're going to realize that He asks you to do just two things: love Him and love other people. When you break down the Ten Commandments, that's really what they're saying. The first four commandments are about loving God and putting Him first. The next six commandments are about how we treat other people. Don't steal their stuff, honor your parents, don't lie, don't be jealous of stuff that other people have. In other words, don't be selfish. Think about other people.

If we're doing those two things with God's help, then we're living the way He wants us to. As you go through the day, try to figure out if you're loving God with your words, thoughts, and actions, and see if you're treating the people around you the way God would want you to—even that kid who sits next to you in homeroom who's being a jerk. Love God and love others. It's pretty simple.

**Extra Credit:** Read Exodus 20:1-17, and see how the Ten Commandments just remind us to love God and love others.

> Dear Lord, thank You that even though following You
> is sometimes hard, it's not complicated. Help me always
> love, honor, and trust You, and please help me love
> other people the way You would. Help me see Your face
> in the face of the ones I have trouble relating to. You
> know who they are. Thanks. In Jesus's name, amen.

Adolescence Fact #645: Middle School students' basic need for adventure often leads them to make questionable decisions.

# 12

## Friends, Feelings, and New Adventures
### How Your Brain Is Growing Up Too

We've been talking about some changes you'll experience during middle school that are easy to see—stuff that naturally happens to your body as it matures.

Meanwhile, there are things going on inside you that you might not even notice, but they're good, and they're all part of God's plans for you. As you reach adolescence, your brain is growing in some cool ways, and your glands are producing new hormones. This will bring some changes in your life that aren't quite so easy to see or measure. You're starting to think and feel in new ways.

### Friend Connections

Middle school brings some social changes. Groups will start to develop that weren't there in elementary school, and some kids will become more popular, while others will kind of retreat into the background. You may be surprised to find out that kids who were your good friends a year ago might not even talk to you now. But the good news is, some kids you didn't even know a year ago might become your new best friends.

People like to be liked, so you may think being popular is

## Helpful Tip: Decide Who to Believe

A few kids might be mean to you or talk rudely. As hard as it is when they act that way, remember that their opinions don't matter at all. They may be loud or big or strong or obnoxious, but they're still kids, just like you. So don't let other people's opinions define who you are. God loves you more than you can imagine because you're one of His kids. And that's the most important thing to remember. Check out 1 John 3:1 and see for yourself.

centered on looks and athletic ability. Truth is, you'll probably be happiest if you don't worry too much about being super popular. It's much more important to have a few good friends.

You might notice in middle school that you're starting to connect in deeper ways with your friends. You might even find yourself pulling away from your parents a little and seeking more approval from your peers. This is okay because you're becoming more independent. You'll always be close to your mom and dad and the rest of your family, but this is the time of your life when you start looking to your friends for more support. Of course, you want to make sure you're making good choices in the friends you hang out with, or you'll find that they'll start influencing you in not-so-good ways (see chapter 10, "Making Friends").

Everybody needs acceptance and approval, and those needs are an even bigger deal during this time, when you're experiencing so many new things. Naturally, your mom is going to say you're beautiful, or your dad will say you're awesome, but you might feel like they sort of have to say those things because they're your parents. (By the way, they really do mean it when they talk that way!) But when a friend compliments you or says you're amazing, that can feel great.

## Strong Feelings!

Between your need for approval and those pesky little emotion hormones flowing through your body and brain, there might be times when you're almost overwhelmed by strong feelings. Some of those emotions feel good, but others...not so much. Not to worry, it's all part of growing up. And God even has a plan for you through all this. Jeremiah 29:11 is a cool promise to hang on to: "'I know the plans I have for you,' says the Lord. 'They are plans for good and not for disaster, to give you a future and a hope'" (NLT). That's exciting, isn't it?

You might find yourself feeling strongly about something that before, like in fourth or fifth grade, you couldn't have cared less about. You might be excited and happy one moment and then sad and depressed the next. A lot of this is happening because your brain is in an important growth stage right now. The cool thing about these new feelings is they make life more exciting and interesting. And probably a little bit dramatic.

One thing to remember is even though feelings can be strong and even overwhelming at times, they're just, well...feelings. They're neither good nor bad—they just *are*. So don't feel bad if you, uh, feel bad.

If you feel like you're up one minute and down the next, or if you start to feel overwhelmed by these strong feelings, try a few of these ideas and see if they help smooth things out a little.

**1. Take a few moments to stop and pray.** You might say something like this: "Lord, I'm not even sure *what* I'm feeling right now, but I need Your help." God knows exactly what you're going through. Sometimes He allows us to go through hard things so we'll learn to rely on and lean on Him more. It's a slow process, but remember, He's in control. He hasn't forgotten you. And He never will.

**2. Take a time-out, slow down, and step back from the situation a little.** For example, if you're stressed about having no friends, take a moment and think about the truth. You've got your family...and how about that kid who sits next to you in English? He seems cool. Also, remember that middle school isn't forever. Things will change as you get older. Sometimes just stepping back helps you see things a bit clearer.

**3. Talk it out.** When things stay inside our heads, they can get all jumbled up. Just saying stuff out loud can help us settle down. It might feel a little scary at first, but sharing a single sentence with someone you trust. "I'm feeling kind of sad today, and I'm not even sure why." You might be surprised how much they appreciate your honesty.

**4. Write it down.** If it's too awkward to talk to your parents, a sibling, or a friend about all these crazy feelings you're experiencing, try this. Grab a notebook or a journal and just write out some of what you're feeling, especially if they're negative feelings. You don't need to show these to anyone—they're just for you. Sometimes putting it on paper helps you understand those strong feelings and takes away some of their intensity.

## Longing for Adventure

As your brain develops during adolescence, you might find yourself longing for excitement and adventure more than when you were younger. You might even be drawn to doing something kind of risky or even dangerous. That's a normal part of your development. What's *not* okay is getting involved in risky behavior, like drinking, using drugs, riding in a car with an irresponsible driver, or trying crazy stunts.

A chemical in your brain called dopamine rewards you with feel-good chemicals whenever you experience something new and exciting. That can be really good...or not so good. So go ahead and try some new and exciting things, like snowboarding, surfing, team sports, mountain biking, or rock climbing. Try out for the talent show or the school play. But think before you do something reckless.

Remember, you're still in a growth stage. You don't want to endanger yourself or anybody else or develop some crazy bad habits that you'll regret later.

## A New Way of Looking at Things

At about this age, you're also going to start noticing that new thoughts and new ways of looking at things will start to develop in that brain of yours. This can be a creative season for you as you come up with new, outside-the-box solutions for the challenges you face. As a little kid, you probably didn't think that much about life's meaning. But as you enter adolescence, you'll start to explore the world around you much more than before. This can lead to a fun, interesting, and exciting life.

The downside of this exploration can be that you might become more open to peer pressure, trying to be someone you're not and doing things that aren't helpful. The most important thing to remember is that you're God's treasure. He knows all about your strengths, your weaknesses, your fears, and your dreams. He loves you more than you can even imagine. Check out what Psalm 139 says:

> O Lord, You have examined my heart and know everything about me. You know when I sit or stand. When far away you know my every thought. You chart the path ahead of me and tell me where to stop and rest. Every moment you know where I am. You know what I am going to say before I even say it (Psalm 139:1-4).

When God is your foundation and you live like you're the most loved person in the universe, you're going to make good choices, have an adventurous life, and pretty much be totally awesome!

---

### Checking In: *Lighten Up!*

---

*Since we are surrounded by such a great cloud
of witnesses, let us throw off everything that
hinders and the sin that so easily entangles.
And let us run with perseverance [patience] the
race marked out for us.*

Hebrews 12:1 NIV

Imagine this scenario: You're at the starting line for the 100-meter dash. All the best runners in the school are lined up with you. But instead of wearing shorts, a T-shirt, and running shoes, you're wearing a long overcoat and a 20-pound backpack. You're carrying a suitcase in one hand and a concrete block in the other. You also have a wide-brimmed hat, beach sandals, and some giant sunglasses. What are you doing!

Pretty dumb scene, huh? Of course, nobody would wear all that stuff to run the 100. Those things would totally weigh you down. But today's Scripture tells us that when we're running the race of

life (like every day), we need to *lighten up*. We can get rid of habits, attitudes, and distractions that aren't going to help us go forward. Stuff like a sour attitude toward a sibling or a friend, not forgiving someone you're mad at, lying, trying to cheat in class or at home, laziness, or getting stuck in anger.

These are the kind of things God wants us to take off and leave behind. He'll help you do it. Ask Him to point out "excess baggage" in your life that's going to slow you down as you go through the day. Learn to lighten up.

**Extra Credit:** Discover what things are weighing you down. Think of some things in your life that are cool—talents, skills, intelligence, friendliness, athletic ability, and so on. List them below under "Strengths."

Now think of some of the things that may be slowing you down—unhelpful habits, an unhealthy attitude toward someone, trouble forgiving someone, laziness—and list them under "Excess Baggage." Be honest and specific. This is just between you and God.

## Strengths

_____

_____

_____

## Excess Baggage

_____

_____

_____

Hi, Lord. I want to live the right way, but sometimes I'm not even sure what excess baggage is slowing me down. Show me if I have any habits or attitudes that aren't helping me grow and be the best I can be. And then give me the power to change those things. Thanks—You're the best. Amen.

# 13

## Your Not-So-Secret Identity
### The Amazing Truth About the Real You

*O my soul, don't be discouraged. Don't be upset.*
*Expect God to act!*

PSALM 42:11

We've seen that middle school can be a time when you start to experience all kinds of new feelings. We've also learned that one of the reasons you might be experiencing strong emotions has to do with all the hormones racing around your body. Hormones help you grow bigger and stronger, but they also help your brain grow, and that sometimes means strong feelings will seem to appear out of nowhere.

We've mentioned that some of those feelings are awesome, but some aren't. Some of the not-so-fun feelings have to do with the way you feel about yourself. Every now and then, you might feel like you're unattractive, out of place, or even a loser. Don't worry, almost all kids feel some of these things, but most never admit it. Here are some of the crazy thoughts that might go through your head:

- "I've got no friends. Nobody likes me."

- "I used to be a cute kid. Now I'm kind of goofy looking. What happened?"

- "I used to be good friends with someone, but now they've turned away from me."

- "I hate my body!"

- "I'm anxious and worried all the time."

- "I wish I were more like _____. Everything seems to go their way."

- "I can't talk to anyone about how lonely I am."

- "I used to get along with my parents, but now all they do is yell and criticize me."

## Self-Esteem: What the Heck Is That?

Those thoughts listed above have to do with self-esteem—how you feel about yourself. How do you feel about the way you look? Or your voice? Or the way you laugh? Are you happy with your athletic ability? Or with how smart you are? That's self-esteem.

If you spend much time on Facebook or Instagram, your self-esteem can take a big-time hit. You go on your computer or your phone and see all your friends having fun. Look! They're in Hawaii or skiing or playing basketball or in a relationship or at a party you didn't even know about! "What? How come I didn't get invited to that?" Online images like those can give you the distorted impression that everybody else's lives are like a Disney movie.

But think about it—with few exceptions, most people don't post when they're bored or doing their homework or feeling lonely or dealing with toe fungus. They post pictures of themselves having fun. So remember this important fact: Facebook (or Instagram) isn't reality. People (especially kids) will take the best photos of themselves having a great time somewhere, and that's what they'll post on social media sites like Facebook, Instagram, or Snapchat. Nobody's life is perfect all the time, no matter what their profile page says.

If social media is starting to get you down or make you depressed, lonely, or angry, you might try taking a break from it. Turn off Facebook, Instagram, and Snapchat for a couple of days or a week. More and more people are doing that. And if you suffer from FOMO (fear of missing out), don't worry—you aren't missing out on anything important. Did you really need to know that Cassie was eating an omelet or Jason was watching *Avengers: Endgame* for the twentieth time? Didn't think so. If something important is going on, your friends will tell you.

We'll talk more about social media in the next chapter.

## Meanwhile, Let's Talk About You

Time to get honest. How do you feel about yourself? Maybe you feel good—got things under control, doing okay in school, got some good friends around, and okay with how things are going. If that's the case, that's great! Take a second to thank God for the good stuff He's doing in your life.

But what if it's not that way? What if you don't like the way you look or think or even sound. What if you think you're too skinny or too fat or not smart enough and this yucky feeling has been going on for a while? What do you do then? Here are seven suggestions:

**1. Take God's word for it.** In His Word—the Bible—He says a lot about who you *really* are. Look up these verses and check it out. He says you're...

> His treasure (Deuteronomy 7:6)
>
> His friend (John 15:15)
>
> His beloved son or daughter (1 John 3:1)
>
> the apple of His eye (Deuteronomy 32:10)

That means He's watching you all the time. You know the way your mom watches you at your soccer game? No matter how many kids are out on the field, she's only watching you. And that's how God is. He also says He's known you since before you were born (Psalm 139:13-16). He's got incredible plans for you that you never ever dreamed of (Jeremiah 29:11). That can make you feel special!

**2. Focus on your strengths.** Figure out the things you do well and focus on those. Do you realize there is nobody on earth who can do exactly what you do? "Really? All I can do is a forward roll or algebra problems or play the trombone or remember all the lines in *Guardians of the Galaxy Vol. 2.*" Yeah that's right! Only you can do that, so celebrate the way God made you!

**3. Find good friends.** Hang around people who build you up rather than put you down. If you find that your friends are making you feel worse rather than better, maybe it's time to slip away from them and spend more time with friends who are better for you. And for that matter, how are *you* talking? Sometimes you might discover that you're joking, teasing, and putting people down just a little too often. You don't have to be a geek, but try to talk positively to others and to yourself.

**4. Start your day right.** Sounds like a commercial for cereal doesn't it? But seriously, if you begin your day by doing something you love—playing with your cat, shooting baskets, listening to your favorite music, drawing, dancing—your mood will be affected and your day will go better. Why not try it for five or ten minutes a day for the next week and see what happens?

**5. Check out the Bible.** You might even start your day by reading a little bit in your Bible. Take five or ten minutes and read some of Matthew, Mark, Luke, or John. Read a chapter from Psalms or Proverbs. We've got 30 short daily readings from the Gospel of Mark at the back of the book to get you started. Let God's Word talk to you every morning.

**6. Talk to yourself.** You might try this little exercise. Every morning when you get up, try saying this yourself, out loud if you can (but if you share a room with your brother or sister, you might want to just say it quietly to yourself): "I feel great about myself. God knows all about me and loves me. 'I can do all things through Christ who strengthens me'" (Philippians 4:13).

**7. Find a helper.** If your sad feelings continue for a week and you're starting to feel depressed, talk to someone about it. You might even consider meeting with a counselor and letting them know what's going on. There are a lot of ways to get free from depression and anxiety, and a professional might be the answer for you.

## Raising Your Parents: Let's Talk

Lots of times your parents won't have any idea of what's going on with you, so even if they want to help out, they can't. Here's a helpful little idea to fix that: Talk to them. Let them know what's going on. They're a lot smarter than they come across. And they love you and want to help you out. Besides, they were in middle school once too, way back when. Talking to them might be a good start in figuring out some of this growing-up stuff.

### Checking In: *A Real BFF*

*There are friends who pretend to be friends, but there is a friend who sticks closer than a brother.*
Proverbs 18:24 RSV

Feeling like a loser—like nobody likes you, nobody cares, and nobody gets you—isn't any fun. Believe it or not, everybody goes through these feelings sometimes, even adults. But hang in there.

These feelings will pass, and as you start to discover who you are—who God created you to be, with distinct and unique gifts and talents that nobody else has—you'll see where you fit in and start to feel a lot better.

In the meantime, try to remember that God loves you. "Oh, sure," you say, "He *has* to because He's God." But His Word says that He's always watching you, He understands exactly what you're going through, and He want to help you. He is your BFF. So go ahead, just ask Him. Say something like, "So God, I'm feeling like a loser today. Nothing's going right. And I'm feeling alone. Can You help me? Help me know that You're there, and show me that You care for me. Thanks. Amen." ("Amen" means "so be it" or "come on, God, make it happen!")

Like we said, feelings come and go, but God's Word stands for all time. Let's go back to some of the feelings we listed at the beginning of this chapter and check out how God's Word answers them.

**Extra Credit:** Read Psalm 42:5. The writer starts out feeling depressed and upset but ends up looking to God for hope. He even thanks God for helping him out. All in one verse!

> Dear Lord, You know me better than I know myself.
> Sometimes I feel all the things on this list, but I also
> know way down in my heart that You love and care
> about me and want me to live in that truth. But I
> need Your help. Please help me know the truth
> about who I am in You. In Jesus's name, amen.

| Sometimes I feel like… | But the Bible assures me… |
|---|---|
| "I've got no friends. Nobody likes me." | "Never will I leave you; never will I forsake you" (Hebrews 13:5 NIV). |
| "I used to be a cute kid. Now I'm kind of goofy looking. What happened?" | "You made all the delicate, inner parts of my body and knit them together in my mother's womb" (Psalm 139:13 NLT). |
| "I used to be good friends with someone, and now they've turned away from me." | "LORD, you have seen this; do not be silent. Do not be far from me, Lord" (Psalm 35:22 NIV). |
| "I hate my body!" | "I praise you, for I am fearfully and wonderfully made" (Psalm 139:14 ESV). |
| "I'm anxious and worried all the time." | "When I am afraid, I put my trust in you" (Psalm 56:3 NIV). |
| "I wish I were more like _____. Everything seems to go their way." | "I know the plans I have for you, says the Lord. They are plans for good and not for evil, to give you a future and a hope" (Jeremiah 29:11). |
| "I can't talk to anyone about how lonely I am." | "Trust in him at all times, you people; pour out your hearts to him" (Psalm 62:8 NIV). |
| "I used to get along with my parents, but now all they do is yell and criticize me." | "Children, obey your parents; this is the right thing to do because God has placed them in authority over you. Honor your father and mother. This is the first of God's Ten Commandments that ends with a promise…And now a word to you parents. Don't keep on scolding and nagging your children, making them angry and resentful. Rather, bring them up with the loving discipline the Lord himself approves, with suggestions and godly advice" (Ephesians 6:1-2,4). |

Liam was beginning to realize just how effective his parents' new filtering software program was.

# 14

## Peer Pressure
### You Can Choose How to Live Your Life

Independence—that can either be a great thing or lead to trouble, depending on what kind of friends you hang out with. Of course, God says we're supposed to love everybody and never judge them, but He also says to use your head when you start making friends: "Do not be misled: 'Bad company corrupts good character'" (1 Corinthians 15:33 NIV).

That means the people you hang out with will influence you for better or for worse. Face it—kids who make bad choices usually encourage good kids to make bad choices along with them. And at your age, some of these bad choices can come back to bite. They can also turn into habits that are hard to break later on. Think: "Is this something I'd like everybody in town to know about? Will this affect my future in a negative way?"

Peer pressure refers to the way the people around you influence your choices. The best way to handle it is to think about it ahead of time. If you wait until you're in a tempting situation to decide how you want to live, you're likely to do what your peers do, not what you believe is right. A smart guy named Josh McDowell says that when we give into any temptation, we stop thinking logically. In fact, we're not thinking at all. So don't get into that situation. Plan ahead.

Right now, take a few minutes to think about how you're going to respond when somebody offers you a cigarette or some alcohol. Or talk with your mom, your dad, or another trustworthy adult about it. What will you do? What will you say when they want you to try some pot or something stronger? What if the boy or girl you like and are spending time with starts to pressure you to go further sexually than you know is right? How do you handle this?

Here are some of the temptations that might come your way and some ideas for how you can respond to them. Write your own response below each one.

**Smoking.** What will you say when some kid you look up to offers you a cigarette? "Hey, no thanks. I don't want to start on the road to lung cancer too soon. I think I'll wait a few years to start hacking and coughing like I've worked in a coal mine all my life."

*What I'll say:*

_____

_____

_____

**Drinking.** Let's say you're at a party or out with friends and someone pulls out a beer and offers it to you. What do you say? "Oh—tempting, but somehow having too much to drink, barfing all over the back seat, and passing out on somebody's lawn doesn't sound like a fun evening to me."

*What I'll say:*

_____

_____

_____

**Drugs.** You might not realize it, but using drugs—even marijuana—is extremely risky for younger people because your brain is still developing. Studies are beginning to show that even drugs like marijuana increase the incidence of some mental illnesses, like schizophrenia, depression, and anxiety. And of course, most drugs are designed to get you hooked, so after a while you can become addicted. So it's best to not even start with them. So what will you say when somebody offers you a joint or something stronger? You might say, "No thanks. Just noticing what happens to my brain when I drink a Mountain Dew is enough for me. Why would I want to lose all rational consciousness and ingest something that some psychopath concocted in his garage? I don't think so."

*What I'll say:*

_____

_____

_____


**Sex.** This one is tricky because there might be a guy or girl that you like, and you may find yourself alone with them and they may want to go further sexually than you know is right. What do you do?

The best thing is to never get in that situation. It's a lot harder to stop when you're alone, the lights are low, and your feelings are running all over the place. To be safe and smart, always meet with members of the opposite sex in public places—at school, a restaurant, or at events where there are lots of people. Much less temptation that way.

*What I'll do:*

_____

_____

_____

**Pornography.** This is another tricky one because porn is everywhere, especially online. And this is one temptation that hits you most often when you're alone. And it's not just guys! If you're finding yourself looking at stuff that you know isn't good, find a friend—a youth pastor, parent, or teacher. Tell them what's happening. Believe it or not, they'll understand. Then ask them to check in on you regularly to make sure you're keeping away from that stuff. You might even have a secret password for what you're talking about: "How are things going at the zoo?" or something like that. Knowing that somebody is there supporting you can make all the difference.

*What I'll do:*

_____

_____

_____

## Dealing with Bullies

This seems like something that happens way too often to way too many kids. You know…a kid who's bigger than you (or maybe just more aggressive) starts using you as a target for his or her anger. And if it keeps going, sometimes you don't even want to come to

Even though a lot of adults believe that kids like you don't think things through, do a lot of dumb stuff, and don't learn from your mistakes, that's not actually true. Recent studies show that most teenagers, even though they may not always use their heads and may end up doing some risky things, *do* learn from their blunders. A lot of teens won't make the same mistake twice.

school anymore. So what do you do? What's the answer? Here are a couple tips that might help.

**1. Show confidence.** Walk and act confidently. Stand up straight and look people in the eye when you're walking down the hall at school. Bullies often pick on kids who are looking down at the floor and seem vulnerable. Show confidence every day.

**2. Avoid them.** As much as possible, stay away from where the bullies hang out. It's too bad schools don't have a "bully area" where only they can hang out and maybe bully each other. But stay away from them if you can. If you need to take a different route to class, do that for a while.

**3. Stay in a group.** This is good advice. Hang around with two or three friends if you're getting harassed by a bully. Bullies will rarely bother someone who's in a group.

**4. Tell someone.** Before the bullying gets so bad that it affects your school day, report it to a teacher. Most schools have strict antibullying policies, and they don't want it happening in their school. If you witness or are the victim of any violence—punching, hitting, kicking, or pushing—this needs to be reported too. Nowadays a lot of schools have anonymous bullying reports on their websites. So go ahead and use them.

*Cyberbullying.* If someone is cyberbullying you—threatening you, insulting you, or making rude remarks about you online— you need to show the message to a parent or teacher and then get offline. Unfriend or block that person so you won't receive their messages. That way they can just send their messages to no one, which is exactly who should be reading them.

## Keeping Safe Online

While we're talking about online stuff, we should mention the internet. You might be online or on your phone right now as you read this. It's the greatest—texting, watching movies, Facebook, Instagram, Snapchat, playing games, keeping up with friends. There are things available now that people wouldn't have even dreamed of ten years ago. There are so many great things about technology, but like everything, there are also some things to look out for. So how do you keep safe and sane online? How do you keep from wrecking your life with a thoughtless post on social media? We might be getting a little carried away, but let's check out four ways you can know you're being safe in the online world.

**1. Don't overshare.** You've probably heard this before, but never share your name, school, address, phone number, or age with a stranger online. In fact, why would you be conversing with a stranger online anyway? Think about it—what would you do if an average Joe you'd never met came up to you on the street and asked, "Hi, what's your name? Where do you go to school? What's your phone number...and while we're at it, where do you live?" Of course, you wouldn't tell him! Creepy. So why would you do it online? If you're playing a game with somebody you don't know, that's understandable, but don't give out your personal information. Duh.

**2. Think ahead.** Before you post something online, like your blog about how you cut class or a rant about a teacher or friend or maybe some inappropriate photo of yourself, just take a moment and think, "What in the world am I doing!" This photo, blog, or mean email, is going to be around the internet until...oh, maybe, *forever*. Yeah, that's right. When you apply for college or a sports team or even when you apply for a summer job, it will be there! So do you want a future coach or college administrator seeing how you cut class or how you complained about a teacher you didn't like? And yes, those adults do check social media. Seventy percent of people hiring for jobs check out applicants' social media pages. Think before you send: "Is this something I'd want my mom or grandma to see?" If not, press delete. See how easy that is?

**3. Avoid inappropriate websites.** You know they're out there. And they're designed to trick you into finding them. In fact, you may have already accidentally clicked on a porn website because it was labeled "recipe for ice cream sundaes" or "how to study for a test." And if you find yourself *purposely* looking for this kind of material, talk to someone about it before it gets out of control. Talk to your dad, mom, youth pastor, or favorite teacher. They'll understand because you're not alone in this. Kids all over the country are struggling with this. But deal with it early before it starts controlling *you*.

## Raising Your Parents: Internet Filters

Your parents can help you find some good and affordable filtering software to keep porn and other junk off your screen and out of your head. Talk to your parents about buying and installing one of these. Check out Qustodio, Net Nanny, Norton Family Premier, or Kaspersky Safe Kids Review.

### Helpful Tip: Don't Buy the Lie

One of the devil's biggest lies to us is this: "You're all alone in this. Nobody struggles with this problem but you, so you better not ever tell anyone about it!" *This is totally untrue!* Think about it—in the history of the world, *not one person* has struggled with the stuff you're dealing with? How much sense does that make? Kids may not say anything, but a lot of them are having trouble with porn or other online stuff, but they don't want to talk about it. When you tell someone, it's like you're turning on the lights. It's no longer in the dark, so it can't hide anymore.

## If You Wouldn't Do It in Person, Don't Do It Online

The thing about the internet is that people can be anonymous—completely unknown. So some people end up doing things and saying things they never would otherwise. You might want to tell off that kid in your science class or that girl on the volleyball team or that totally unfair teacher. You might even want to do a little cyberbullying. But before you do, you need to *think ahead*. Is that who

### Cell Phone Smarts

Want a simple hack that'll help you sleep better, lower your chance of depression, and even help you with self-esteem? Don't sleep with your cell phone.

Studies show that kids who sleep with their cells within reach sleep less and experience more depression and lower self-esteem. Some kids even text in their sleep! Set your own curfew and turn off your phone or put it in a drawer at least a half hour before you go to bed. Don't believe us? Try it for a couple of weeks and see if you start feeling better.

One thing you don't want to do is text something inappropriate (including photos of your body, swearing, a rant about a teacher or kid at school) to anyone. There are thousands of stories of kids who texted something to a friend that they didn't want to get out, and...well, it did. You've heard of going viral? That's what might happen—and not in a good way. Be smart. Think. Once something's out there, you're never going to get it back.

you want to be? There are so many ways to deal with relational conflict that are better than ranting online. If you need to rant, then try this: Get on there and type all the things you want to say. Rant, yell, complain...all that stuff. Then *please* press delete. We promise you—you'll be so glad you did.

## Checking In: *Looking Down the Road*

> Don't be misled; remember that you can't ignore
> God and get away with it: a man will always
> reap [harvest] just the kind of crop he sows!
> Galatians 6:7

One of the definitions of maturity or growing up is being able to look down the road and see the outcome of our actions today. In other words, being able to see how what we're doing right now will affect us in a week, a month, or a couple of years.

For example, if you eat nothing but candy bars and soft drinks every day, you might not be in great shape when you try out for a sports team. Or if you post something online that's stupid or mean, it could come back to bite you, even in a few years.

True story: A guy in his twenties had a chance to star in a TV show a couple of years ago. It was his big break! It was a cool show about racial reconciliation (everybody getting along). Then people discovered that when he was 13 or 14 years old, he posted an awful racist rant online, never thinking it would ever affect anything. You guessed it—he was fired from the TV show.

Learn from his lesson. Think ahead! Even though God loves you and promises to forgive your sins, when we do dumb stuff, we usually must experience the consequences. Before you do something that might be hurtful to you or to other people, stop for a second and ask yourself, "How is this going to affect me in the future?" Look down the road.

**Extra Credit:** Take a couple of minutes and write down some areas where your actions now might affect your life in the future. Think about things like sex, drugs, fighting, and online stuff. Be honest. What are some areas you can think of?

> Dear Lord, I don't think that much about the future. I need
> Your help to think that way sometimes, especially when
> I'm making important decisions. Help me include You in my
> planning and to be smart in my decision-making. Amen.

# 15

## Being Friends with Christ
### Heaven, God, and His Plans for You

What do *you* think about God? Not your parents, but you? You might not think about it very often, but God wants you to get to know Him and to discover His plans for your life. When you were little, you probably just went along with what your parents felt about God...if they felt anything about Him at all. But now that you're older, you might be feeling like you want to decide for yourself.

You also might be having some doubts about this whole God thing. "Is He real? Some of the stories I've heard from the Bible seem a little far-fetched. Like a fish swallowing a guy? A kid fighting a giant? Jesus walking on water? I mean, is all this real? What's the truth here?"

Maybe you've gone to church with your parents, attended Sunday school, or joined a youth group, but God wants something even better. He wants to begin a personal relationship with you. What does that mean, you might ask?

Here's the deal. God created everything, including all of us. And even though He made the Grand Canyon, the Atlantic Ocean, the tropics, Hawaii, and Chicago, His favorite thing is *you*. That's right—you.

But (and this is a big but) we all do bad stuff. Think about it. Have you ever said anything, done anything, or even *thought* anything (uh-oh) that hurt another person or even yourself? Join the club. So here's God (perfect, holy, pure), and then here we are (imperfect, to put it mildly). So how can we live together?

We can't.

So God made a plan to forgive us and get us all back together. He figured that the sin (the bad stuff we do) had to be punished. But this was some big punishment because it was for the whole world—everybody who's ever messed up, which is pretty much all of us.

So Jesus, God's Son, came and lived a perfect life among us. Think about that for a minute. A perfect life. He never did, said, or

Look at Madison, I wish I were more like her.
She's got it all together.

Look at Aurora, I wish I were more like her.
She's got it all together.

Adolescence Fact # 721
Everyone thinks everyone else has it all together.

even thought anything wrong. Whoa. And then when Jesus was 33, His friends deserted Him, and a bunch of His enemies captured Him and sold Him out to the Roman government.

The Romans' punishment for the crime they accused Jesus of was crucifixion. Even though Jesus was innocent, they nailed Him to the cross and let Him hang there all day long. We call that day Good Friday. But being whipped, beaten, spit upon, and nailed to the cross wasn't even the worst part. While Jesus was on the cross, God the Father turned His back on Jesus, His only Son. Since Jesus was carrying all our sin on Himself, He was separated from God that day so we don't ever have to be.

And then three days later, Jesus proved He was who He said He was and was raised from the dead. And He's still alive! Whoa.

But just because Jesus did all that doesn't mean it automatically becomes ours. We need to receive it. It's like somebody giving you a birthday present—it isn't yours unless you receive it and open it, right? So if you want to begin a relationship with God, you need to do the same thing with the gift He has for you. Receive this gift of being reconnected with God. It's easy, but you've got to ask from your heart. Here is a way to start the process that's as simple as *ABC*.

1. **A**dmit you've messed up. You're like the rest of us—we've all done some bad stuff. We're guilty, and we need someone to take the punishment for us.

2. **B**elieve that Jesus is who He says He is—God's Son who came to show us the Father as well as die on the cross for our sake.

3. **C**onfess that you want Jesus to be your Lord (boss) and Savior (the One who took your punishment). This is how you start a relationship with Him. And it's truly the most important decision you'll ever make in your life. Like any friendship, you'll grow to know Jesus more and more every day as you spend time with Him, pray, read His Word, and get together with kids and adults who love God and love you.

See? That's pretty much all you need to know to get started. Cool, huh?

But what if you have questions and doubts about this whole God business? Well, as you enter your teen years, you'll find that you'll start to question a lot of things that you just assumed were true when you were younger. That's okay. That's called thinking. And it's okay to have questions and doubts about your faith. Even Jesus's disciples—the people who lived with him for a few years—felt that way sometimes. Check out Matthew 28:17 (NIV): "When they saw [Jesus] they worshipped Him; but some doubted." Wow. If these men and women who had seen Jesus heal sick people, walk on water, and even raise a guy from the dead had doubts, I guess it's normal for us to question things too.

God wants us to bring our questions and doubts to Him and trust Him. Trust that He cares about us and wants us to get to know Him. That's what faith is. It's trusting God.

If you asked your mom or dad or a good friend for a favor and they said they'd do it, you'd trust them to do it, right? You'd have faith in them that they would do what they said. Well, that's what having faith in God is. Trusting that He is who He says He is and that He loves you.

So it's okay to ask questions. In fact, it's good to study the Bible, talk to older Christians, and ask God to reveal Himself to you. He'll do it. Whether you're starting middle school or just hanging with friends, He's always there with you.

## FAQs About God and Faith

### 1. If God is so good and powerful, why do bad things like wars, famines, shootings, and child abuse happen? Why does He allow it?

Here's the thing. When Adam and Eve disobeyed God, their disobedience affected the entire earth. Now instead of living in a perfect world, we live in a fallen, stained one. Natural disasters, such as earthquakes, floods, fires, and tsunamis, continue all over the world. People hurt other people. God gave us a free will—the choice to follow Him or not. And when we don't follow Him, we can end up doing all kinds of bad stuff. The good news for Christians is that no matter what we go through, God will stay right by our side. And sometimes when we go through bad stuff, God will use it to draw us closer to Him.

### 2. Is there a devil?

Yes, the Bible and Jesus teach that the devil (also called Satan) is an actual being who, like an angel, is invisible but nonetheless very real. His goal is to disrupt the plans of God and God's people, but God is much more powerful than Satan. If we're walking with Jesus, we don't need to fear the devil.

### 3. Is there a heaven and a hell?

Yes, heaven is a place where Jesus and God the Father live, and it will be the dwelling place for all people who put their trust in Jesus. It's a place of eternal joy and fellowship with God as well as all the people who love Him. Hell is a place originally designed for Satan and his followers, but now it also houses all the people who have rejected Jesus's offer of life. If you follow Jesus, you won't be going there. Jesus talked more about hell than a lot of other things He taught about in the New Testament.

### 4. What about the people who have never heard of Jesus? Do they automatically go to hell?

We need to remember two things regarding this question. One is that it's not up to us to decide who's going to heaven and who's going to hell. That's God's job. The second thing to remember is that God is perfect, fair, and just. He sees what's going on in each person's heart. We can totally trust that He's going to make the right decision regarding every person. The Bible also says that God reveals Himself to everyone in different ways, including through the beauty of nature and through something inside each one of us that tells us there's someone bigger than us out there (check out Romans 1:20). So even people who haven't ever heard the good news of Jesus Christ still have a chance to respond to what they have known of God.

### 5. If I mess up, do I lose my relationship with God?

Every person on earth does bad stuff, even Christians. So the answer is no. When we mess up, we need to go to God and tell Him we're sorry. If we confess our sin, He will forgive us (1 John 1:9). The only way we lose our relationship with God is by completely turning our back on Him, rejecting Him, and basically saying "I want nothing to do with You!" (But many people have done that and then come back to the Lord later.) The best thing for you to do to stay close to God is to grow with Jesus every day. Ask for His help in the areas where you feel tempted, read His Word, and hang around other kids who are growing in Him too. If you do that, you'll not only get to know Him better but might just end up changing the world!

## Checking In: *You Might Have to Be Weird*

> *Don't let the world around you squeeze you into its own mold, but let God re-mold your minds from within.*
>
> Romans 12:2 PHILLIPS

As you begin to grow in your relationship with God, there might be times when you'll have to decide: "Do I go along with my friends and do something I know isn't right, or do I stand up and look weird to them?"

Now, God doesn't want you to go around telling other people how bad they are or using Bible verses to put people down. We're supposed to live our lives in a good and kind way. But occasionally you'll come up against something that you know won't honor God. It might be in a class where the teacher is saying things like the Bible isn't true or at a party when some friends want you to drink or smoke with them. It might show up in the kinds of movies your friends want to watch or games they want to play.

But remember, it's not about making a list of good and bad things; it's about listening to God. If you're feeling uneasy about something you're about to do, it might be God's Spirit inside you alerting you.

So what do you do? Well first, slow down and ask Him what He wants you to do or not do. In a class, you might need to talk to the teacher privately later and let them know where you stand regarding your faith. If it's at a party, you may need to get out of there, or just say, "No thanks." You might feel, look, or sound weird to your friends, but it's totally worth it to follow God. Sometimes you might have to be weird.

## Wrapping Up

"Wow, that's a lot of stuff to remember! My brain is ready to explode!" you exclaim. Well, we warned you. It's a ton of info to take in regarding all this middle school stuff, but keep this book around as a reference and check back with it every so often. That way, you'll soon become an actual world-class expert on the topic. We know that there are probably still some things we might have left out, but hopefully this book has helped you prepare for this wonderful, wacky, crazy, and important time in your life.

## An Awesome Five-Minute Bible-Reading Plan
### 30 Days in the Gospel of Mark

Here is a simple, realistic (meaning not too long), 30-day Bible reading plan. Hopefully this will get you in the habit of reading God's Word for five or ten minutes a day. We're starting in the book of Mark in the New Testament, near the back of your Bible. We skip some sections in our reading plan, but feel free to read them too if you want. If you don't have a Bible, talk to your parents about getting one. Some inexpensive paperback versions are available at bookstores or online. You can also Google "Bible" / "Gospel of Mark" on your computer or phone, and you should get the whole thing right there. So try this: Read the bible passage listed, go through the short paragraph for explanations, and then answer the questions. You might want to write down your thoughts in a notebook or journal.

### Day 1
**Read Mark 1:1-11**

Did you know that John the Baptist was Jesus's cousin? Check out Luke 1:36. God called John to prepare the way for Jesus by preaching and baptizing people in the Jordan River in Israel. One day Jesus came to John to be baptized. As Jesus came up out of the water, God's Spirit came down on Him in the form of a dove, and God spoke from heaven.

What did He say?

## Day 2

**Read Mark 1:12-13**

Jesus spent 40 days in the wilderness being tempted by the devil. But Jesus resisted all the devil's temptations. He knew He had to obey God to be our perfect sacrifice.

What's an area in your life where you have felt tempted?

## Day 3

**Read Mark 1:14-20**

After Jesus's time in the wilderness, He went up to the northern part of Israel to the Sea of Galilee. There, He invited four fishermen to leave their boats and follow Him.

What were the names of the four fishermen? Why do you suppose they left everything and followed Jesus?

## Day 4

**Read Mark 1:21-28**

The people who heard Jesus teach said He taught with authority. (You think?) Of course, they didn't know He was God's Son at the time. Jesus also showed His authority by casting an unclean spirit out of a man.

What would you have thought if you had been there and witnessed that?

## Day 5

**Read Mark 1:29-34**

Now Jesus starts into His healing ministry. First, He healed Peter's mother-in-law, and then He healed tons of people that evening.

In a time when there were few doctors around, how do you think the people responded to this display of God's power?

## Day 6
### Read Mark 1:40-45

In today's reading, we meet a man who had leprosy—an incurable disease that slowly ate away people's bodies. We don't have much of this disease around anymore. The guy knew that Jesus was powerful enough to heal him, but he wasn't sure that Jesus would care enough to.

What was Jesus's response? Do you sometimes feel like God is so big He couldn't possibly care about you? That's not true. He loves you and knows everything about you.

## Day 7
### Read Mark 2:1-12

Jesus was becoming so popular that crowds followed Him wherever He went. At this point, He's inside someone's house (it might have been Peter's), and the mob was so big that people outside even pressed in around the windows and doors.

How do you think these four guys and their paralyzed friend felt when they saw the crowd? Most people would have given up and gone home. What would you have done?

## Day 8
### Read Mark 2:13-17

Jesus had already recruited some fishermen to follow Him, and now He was asking a tax collector to join up. Back then, tax collectors were hated by almost everyone because they worked for the Roman government (Israel's enemy).

What was the response of the religious leaders when Jesus invited Levi (also known as Matthew) to join in? What was Jesus's answer to them?

## Day 9
### Read Mark 2:18-22

Back in Jesus's day, the Jewish people sometimes fasted (went without food) from dawn to dusk. But Jesus's disciples didn't fast, and the religious leaders wanted to know why. Jesus basically told them that while He was with them, they didn't need to fast. They could do that later. When He talked about the wineskins, He was saying that He was bringing something completely new (the Christian faith) to the world, and to try to tack that onto the Jewish traditions was like putting new wine (which expands) into old, inflexible wineskins.

What changes has Jesus brought to your life?

## Day 10
### Read Mark 3:1-6

In today's reading, Jesus gets confronted about the Sabbath. He calls a man with a withered hand up in front of the entire synagogue (this was the religious gathering place of the Jewish people). Would He heal the man on the day of rest?

How did Jesus respond to the question? (See verse 4.) Then what did Jesus do?

## Day 11
### Read Mark 3:7-19

These verses contain a lot of Jesus's activities in a short time. He traveled around, taught huge crowds, and healed lots of people. He also chose His 12 closest disciples. You'll find all their names in verses 16-19. All these men (except Judas) would go out and, with Jesus's Spirit inside them, change the world.

Imagine Jesus choosing you to do a special task. What might it be?

## Day 12

### Read Mark 3:20-35

In this section, Jesus gets some major pushback, even from His own family (verse 21). Some of the religious leaders even accused Jesus of working with the devil!

Have you ever been misunderstood or accused of doing something you didn't do? Jesus wants us to be united in our families, with friends, and especially with other Christians. Is someone in your life coming against you? What can you do to help heal the division and promote unity?

## Day 13

### Read Mark 4:1-9

In these verses, we hear Jesus share one of His first parables. A parable is a short story with a strong lesson. In this parable, He talks about a farmer who's out throwing seeds in a field. How many kinds of ground were there? In the next ten verses, Jesus takes time to explain the story to His disciples. We'll look at His explanation tomorrow.

## Day 14

### Read Mark 4:10-20

Today Jesus explains what His parable was all about. He says that the seeds the farmer was throwing out was the Word of God. He says that the different types of ground represent the different ways people respond to God's Word.

Take a look at the list and see which kind of "ground" you are. God wants us all to grow up and be like the good ground that receives His Word and starts to bear fruit.

## Day 15

### Read Mark 4:35-41

In today's reading, we see that the disciples' view of Jesus grew tremendously. They thought they knew Him. Good guy, teacher, prophet...and He even healed people a lot. But what do you think they thought when Jesus stood up and commanded the weather—and it obeyed Him?

In what ways has your view of Jesus changed in the past year or so?

## Day 16

### Read Mark 5:21-34

This is the first half of a cool story. A wealthy leader named Jairus comes to Jesus and asks him to heal his daughter. But on the way, an unknown woman (notice they never even tell us her name) reaches out and touches Jesus's robe. And she's instantly healed. That's great, but can you imagine Jairus's frustration when Jesus sits down and listens to her whole story (verse 33)?

Have you ever had to wait for God to answer your prayer? Maybe you're still waiting. How does that make you feel? Can you relate to Jairus? We'll discover the rest of the story tomorrow.

## Day 17

### Read Mark 5:35-43

In today's reading, we pick up where we left off yesterday. Jesus is on the way to Jairus's house when they get the message that the little girl has died. But Jesus isn't discouraged. He tells Jairus to keep believing. When they get to the house, Jesus makes everyone leave. Then He, Peter, James, John, the mom, and Jairus enter the girl's room—and Jesus brings the girl back to life.

Do you have a situation in your life right now that looks impossible? Tell God all about it. Jesus is the Lord of the impossible.

## Day 18

### Read Mark 6:7

"And Jesus sent them out two by two." Interesting. He was training His disciples to go out and share the good news that He had come into the world. But did you notice? He didn't send them out by themselves. He sent them out two by two. They had a friend.

Have you ever noticed how much easier it is to do stuff when you've got another person alongside you? They can encourage and support you, and you can do the same for them. If you don't have a friend like that, ask God to send you one who will help you grow in your friendship with Him.

## Day 19

### Read Mark 6:30-44

Have you ever been really hungry, and all you could think about was what you were going to eat? Well, these people—more than 5,000 of them—were in that situation. They'd been out on the hill-side all day, far away from their homes or even a market. And Jesus decided to feed them with five miniature loaves of bread and two fish!

Who do you think were more surprised by this miracle—the people Jesus fed or the disciples? When we read this story, we realize that God is interested in every little detail of our lives, including what's for dinner.

## Day 20

### Read Mark 6:45-48

In this story, Jesus sends His disciples off in a boat to cross the Sea of Galilee while He goes up on the mountain to pray. Who was He praying for? Maybe it was the 5,000 people He just fed with the fish and the loaves. Or maybe He was praying for His friends out in the storm on the lake. Verse 48 says that He could see them struggling and trying to get to the other side.

Did you know that God sees you all the time? When you're struggling or scared or lonely or even when you're celebrating! God sees you—all the time.

## Day 21
**Read Mark 6:49-52**

This is the second half of the story we started yesterday. Jesus's disciples are in the middle of a storm on the Sea of Galilee—and it was a big one. They thought they were going to sink! So what does Jesus do? He breaks His own laws of nature and walks out on the water to reach them.

We can learn from this story that God will do whatever it takes to get to you when you need Him. Even break His own natural laws! Can you think of a situation recently where you could have used God's help? What did you do?

## Day 22
**Read Mark 7:31-37**

One thing you'll notice about Jesus as you read through the Gospels is that He rarely heals people the same way twice. When they brought a deaf man who couldn't speak properly to Jesus, how did He heal him? Could this be a sign that we're never going to fully understand God and His ways?

Is there something that happened in your life a while back that now, looking back, you can see how God was involved?

## Day 23
**Read Mark 8:22-26**

In this story, we see Jesus healing a blind man. Again, Jesus does something different—He spits on the guy's eyes! That had to be a shock to the blind man. And then Jesus does another interesting thing—He asks the man if he can see anything. The man's vision had improved, but it was still blurry. He saw people walking around, but they looked like walking trees. So Jesus put His hands on the guy again and told him to look up. This time he was healed! He could see everything clearly!

Why do you suppose it took two times for Jesus to heal this guy's blindness? Could it be that God is saying that some healings take time?

## Day 24

### Read Mark 8:27-30

Jesus's disciples were learning more and more about Jesus every day. They'd seen Him feed 5,000 people with a few fish and some bread. They'd seen Him calm the sea, and they'd seen Him heal all kinds of sick people instantly. So when Jesus asks them who people think He is, they answered that people thought He was John the Baptist raised from the dead or Elijah (who also did lots of miracles) or another prophet from the Old Testament. But then Jesus asks them who *they* thought He was. Peter answers and says, "You're the Christ, the One that God sent." Peter was starting to figure out that Jesus wasn't just a great prophet. He was the Son of God, come to earth.

Who would you say Jesus is to you?

## Day 25

### Read Mark 8:31-38

Jesus gets serious with His disciples in this section. He tells them that His kingdom isn't about political power but that He is going to Jerusalem to suffer and die. And then He tells them that they need to set their eyes on eternal things and not just the things of this world. That's deep.

Are there things in your life that might be too important to you? God doesn't want us to go without friends, fun activities, or possessions. But He does know that we get in trouble when these things begin to mean more to us than our friendship with Jesus.

## Day 26
### Read Mark 9:1-13

In this passage, Jesus and three of His closest disciples—Peter, James, and John—go up to the top of a mountain. When they get there, Jesus is transfigured before their eyes. Wait, what? What does that mean? It's like the three disciples get to catch a small glimpse of who Jesus is—not just a cool teacher and friend. He really is the Son of God! Two Old Testament heroes of the faith, Moses and Elijah, appear with Him. It must have been a crazy moment. But then God speaks from heaven and says to listen to Jesus, meaning that Jesus is higher than all and is to be honored. Whew, what a day.

What do you think you would have said if you had seen Jesus shining on the mountain?

## Day 27
### Read Mark 9:14-27

When Jesus and His three friends come down from the mountain, they run into a father whose son is filled with an evil spirit that causes convulsions and keeps the boy from speaking. The man asks Jesus to heal his son but says, "I believe, help my unbelief!" What an honest guy. And guess what? Jesus answered that prayer for that dad.

Have you ever felt that like that dad? "I believe Jesus, but not totally. Please help me believe in You." Do you think Jesus healing the boy helped the dad's unbelief from that moment on? Guess so! Is there something going on with you right now that you'd like to ask Jesus to help you with? Let Him know about it and ask Him to help your unbelief.

## Day 28

**Read Mark 9:30-37**

Busted! Jesus caught the disciples arguing about which one of them was the greatest. Awkward. So check out what Jesus does. He doesn't get mad or even call them out on their silly dispute. He says that with Him, things are completely upside down from this world. The great ones are like little kids, trusting and believing and taking the time to serve other people. That's completely opposite of how most of the world operates.

Is there someone in your life right now that you could serve? Is it hard? What's a small thing you can do for them?

## Day 29

**Read Mark 10:13-16**

A lot of people believe that God is too busy with the big stuff going on in the world—you know, like wars and earthquakes—to be bothered with their problems. But this Scripture shows that God is interested in everyone. Back then, kids weren't valued. So when some parents brought their children to see Jesus, the disciples tried to shoo them away. But Jesus corrected this thinking and told the disciples to let the kids come and see Him.

We all need to be like children when we come to Jesus. Kids trust, believe, and obey a lot better than most adults. How about you? How have you trusted Jesus as if you were a little kid? That's the kind of faith He wants from us.

## Day 30

**Read Mark 10:17-27**

The guy in this story seems genuinely sincere in wanting to do the right thing. He was trying to follow all God's commandments, but Jesus saw that the guy's heart still wasn't right. He was being good, but something was more important than his relationship with

Jesus. Can you tell what it was? Check out verse 22 for a hint. Even though he was trying to follow all the rules, this guy wasn't ready to give up the things that were important to him.

What are some things that could get in the way of people following Jesus with their whole heart?

# More Great Harvest House Books for Kids
# by Sandy Silverthorne

### Awesome Book of Bible Comics
Bible stories can be seriously awesome! *The Awesome Book of Bible Comics* illustrates many of the most popular stories from the Bible. Jump in and see how God showed His love and faithfulness through each of these adventures.

### Awesome Coloring Book of Bible Comics
Add your own color and captions to the most exciting stories from the Bible, making this fun comic book your very own unique creation. Get ready to experience the Bible's most action-packed adventures!

### Wild and Wacky Bible Adventures for Kids
Children ages 6 to 12 will instantly relate to these up-to-date retellings of Bible stories and comical illustrations. Sandy pairs biblical accounts with contemporary technology and culture. These stories will captivate young minds and hearts while maintaining the integrity of the message.

### Awesome Book of Bible Facts
A storybook, first Bible dictionary, and gold mine of fascinating facts all in one. It's packed with amazing information, incredible cut-away diagrams, hundreds of illustrations, and short, easy explanations kids will love.

# And for the Whole Family...

### Amazing Tips to Make You Smarter

Loaded with fun, offbeat trivia, and Sandy Silverthorne's hilarious cartoons, this book will make you smarter and much more fun to be around. Who wouldn't want to hear which two first-world countries haven't signed a treaty to end WWII or where the phrase "a blue moon" came from?

### Two Truths and a Tall Tale

Looking for something to get your family unplugged from their devices and engaged in some lively discussion? Indulge their love of trivia and fun facts with this unique game book of fact versus fiction.

### The Very Best One-Minute Mysteries and Brain Teasers

Put on your detective hat and prepare to solve the best mindbenders from the popular One-Minute Mysteries series. This collection of crazy conundrums will keep you guessing until the final page and provide fun for detectives of all ages.

To learn more about Harvest House books and
to read sample chapters, visit our website:

**www.harvesthousepublishers.com**

HARVEST HOUSE PUBLISHERS
EUGENE, OREGON